To Faank
Michael H

A Journey to Station X

Michael A Kushner

www.michaelkushner.co.uk

MMXV VIII

For

Angela 1949 -2004
Valerie 1953 -2014

A Journey to Station X

Michael Kushner is a volunteer guide & Lecturer at Bletchley Park, the British Government's World War II ultra top secret code-breaking establishment, known as War Station X. Before 1980 very few people knew of its existence and how important a part that Bletchley played during the Second World War. This is where the German secret cipher machines Enigma and Lorenz were broken. Bletchley Park employed some of the top British brains to develop procedures and equipment to break these top secret codes. Michael tells the fascinating story of how we broke into the German U-boat, *Luftwaffe*, army and Naval codes. Also how we invented the world's first electronic digital computer Colossus, used for the first time at Bletchley Park to de-cipher the Lorenz cipher machine. This machine was being used to send high grade intelligence including Adolf Hitler's most secret battle plans to his generals. All the staff that worked at Bletchley Park was sworn to absolute secrecy, but now this story can be told, which as historians tell us shortened the war by at least two years and saved countless lives.

Information

Thank you for choosing my book, which depicts an historical record of events regarding signals intelligence up to and throughout World War II the pages reflect my research and lectures which I give for many organisations, including the world famous cruise lines. These lectures are normally accompanied with a PowerPoint presentation. Through the pages I have tried to bring the following text to life. However though I have attempted via the National archives at Kew, the British library St Pancras in London, also with the help of many respected historical publications to be as accurate as possible, it could be that some references and dates are out of sequence. I have tried to avoid this, but the book is designed to accompany my talks rather than an historical research document. I am thankful to the following people for help and assistance with this publication: Danielle B Kushner, Paul J Kushner, Zvi Friedman, Susan Walker-Rosten, I have also listed in the bibliography the much respected publications that I have used and can be used for serious historical research and reference. Of these mentioned books to the authors and publishers I am gratefully indebted.

Michael A Kushner

Index

Introduction

In 1974, with the publication of the book by Group Captain Frederick Winterbotham "The Ultra secret", it was revealed that during World War II absolute top-secret work was being carried out at a Victorian mansion in the North Buckinghamshire town of Bletchley. The work in question was the breaking of German codes and ciphers. In this small Buckinghamshire railway town, it has been revealed that at the height of its operation, Bletchley Park employed close to 10,000 staff. Everyone who worked at this establishment was sworn to absolute secrecy, staff had to sign the Official Secrets Act. No one lived on-site. Staff were billeted out to hotels, bed-and-breakfasts, pubs and lodgings. Some staff were even housed in the stately home of Woburn Abbey in Bedfordshire just 8 miles away.

Whilst 85% of the 10,000 personnel working at Bletchley Park were military, there was no marching up and down, square-bashing or saluting. Only a few wore the uniform correctly, if at all. It was merely a formality. But of the military personnel, 75% were ladies of the ATS, RAF (WAFS), and the women's Royal Naval service WRNS or Wrens as they were known.

In this book we will be talking about the brilliant work of the code-breakers, and of the fantastic job they did in breaking the German ciphers and codes such as the Enigma and Lorenz machines, including Japanese and Italian systems, which many were deemed impossible to crack. But if it wasn't for the thousands of dedicated ladies mainly Wrens who worked on the labour-intensive and at times boring, administration, the operation of code-breaking would have not been the success it was. They operated a shift pattern at Bletchley: From 8am to 4pm, from 4am until midnight and from midnight to 8am, usually in quite poor working conditions. Bletchley Park also supported by out-stations in Stanmore, Middlesex; Eastcote, Middlesex; and overseas. This book will give you an insight as to how Bletchley Park operated and its contribution to the downfall of Adolf Hitler.

A brief history of code-breaking

When we think of code-breaking, we might well think of the people of Bletchley Park and its now well-known efforts in cracking war-time codes. But let's take a look at code-breaking a little further back in history.

Egyptians

The Rosetta Stone is a granodiorite stele inscribed with a decree issued at Memphis, Egypt in 196 BC on behalf of King Ptolemy V. The decree appears in three scripts: the upper text is Ancient Egyptian hieroglyphs, the middle portion Demotic script, and the lowest is in Ancient Greek. Because it presents essentially the same text in all three scripts (with some minor differences among them), it provided the key to the modern understanding of Egyptian hieroglyphs. The Stone, which was found in the town of Rosetta in the Nile Delta in 1799, is in fact a code-book. By using the languages we know and comparing them with the hieroglyphics, we were able to establish the meanings of these ancient Egyptian symbols.

Ancient Greeks

It has been alleged that the Greek Philosopher Plato (348/347 BC) hid secret codes within musical staves. These hidden codes suggest that Plato anticipated the Scientific Revolution 2,000 years before Isaac Newton. Plato uncovered its most important concept that nature is written in the language of mathematics. By decoding these messages some surprising insights that unite the sciences are opened up.

Romans

In cryptography, a Caesar cipher, or the shift cipher is one of the simplest and most widely-known encryption techniques. It is a type of substitution cipher in which each letter in the plaintext is replaced by a letter some fixed number of positions down the alphabet. For example, with a left shift of 3, D would be replaced by A, E would become B, and so on. The method is named after Julius Caesar, who used it to send secret messages to his legions across the Roman Empire, as well as for his private correspondence.

Tudors

In Tudor times, which it is said was the start of British secret intelligence, Sir Francis Walshingham, the Secretary of State to Queen Elizabeth uncovered a plot to overthrow the crown. In 1585 Anthony Babbington was communicating with Mary Queen of Scots, by way of secret messages delivered in the stoppers of beer barrels to the prison at Chartley Hall Staffordshire, where Mary was incarcerated. The coded messages were intercepted by Walshingham and his spy-masters, resulting in Mary's execution.

Journey to Station X

At the turn of the 20th century, communications between countries was by the use of under-sea telegraph cables. The cable companies were mainly British, as in the Eastern Telegraph Company, the Marconi Company, and the General Post Office (GPO). Radio, though in its infancy, was what the great navies of the world were using to communicate. Just after hostilities of World War 1 commenced on 14th August 1914, GPO cable ships *CS Alert & CS Telconia* sailed into the North Sea, and grappled up many of the cables that connected Germany with the rest of the world. By severing these cables, Germany was forced to use radio communication.

Many of Germany's signals were now being intercepted by the Admiralty, and they appeared to be in code. Owing to Britain being at war, the Admiralty decided to set up a department which would be responsible for intercepting and decoding these messages. Admiral Henry Oliver, the Director of Naval intelligence (DNI), contacted his friend and colleague James Ewing, the director of naval education, based at the Royal Naval College at Greenwich. Ewing contacted all the naval colleges around the country seeking an expert in the German language. Eventually he located Alistair Denniston, a lecturer at the Royal Naval College at Osborne in the Isle of Wight, who fitted the bill perfectly. For Denniston this was the early beginnings of a career that would take him through World War 1 and beyond.

A department was set up at the Old Admiralty Buildings in London just adjacent to Trafalgar Square. It was located in a small room, number 40. The 1st Lord of the Admiralty was also involved with the creation of Room 40 in 1914: that position was held by Winston Churchill. The official name for the new department was Naval Intelligence Department 25 (NID 25). As the war continued larger rooms were needed for interception and code-breaking, but the name stuck and the whole department remained known as Room 40 By 1915, Room 40 had had some success with intercepting and breaking German messages, but then came a real breakthrough.

Capture of the SKM *(signalbuch der Kaiserlichmarine)* code book. *SMS Magdeburg*, a fast mine-laying German torpedo ship, had orders to sail to the Baltic and into a Russian port. Once there, it was to lay mines, torpedo as many Russian ships as possible, then make its escape. Which it did. The *Magdeburg* thought it had got away, but in thick fog its crew made an error of navigation and on 26th August 1914 she ran aground on a sandbank. With the Russian Navy on their tail, the Magdeburg forwarded and reversed engines in desperation, but it was hopeless. Ordered to remove any weighty items, the crew threw overboard railings, bulk-head doors, and even ammunition. As the fog cleared, the Russian ships came into view and the Magdeburg was in clear-sight, stuck in the sandbank. In the shallow waters of the Baltic, shipping has to follow a very narrow channel. This misjudgment had cost the vessel dearly, and the Captain's efforts to free it were proving futile. It was decided by Captain Habenicht to scuttle the Magdeburg. The crew hastily placed the scuttling charges around the ship, and set them to detonate. However, this was not the instruction: they were only supposed to place the charges and await further orders. When the Captain Habenicht realised the error, the crew were quickly ordered to abandon ship as it was about to explode in 4 ½ minutes. Protecting the secret papers and code-books was paramount. The concern was that if the enemy boarded the ship, or whatever remained of it, they may find the secret documents. With no crew able to save the documents, the Captain knew that they had to be destroyed. He grabbed the code-books and jumped over the side, the sea at that point was only ten to fifteen feet deep. The Magdeburg then blew up and was ripped apart. Captain Habenicht's intentional suicidal plan was to take himself and the code-books to the bottom. When the Russian ships caught up with the Magdeburg, they found Captain Habenicht standing up to his waist in water, hugging the books.

The Russians took the surviving crew as prisoners of war and took the sopping wet cipher key books back to St Petersburg. As Russia was an ally to Britain in the war, they decided to make copies of the code- book and personally deliver them to the 1st Lord of the Admiralty in London, that being Winston Churchill.

Capture of the HVB *(Handelsverkehrsbuch)* code book was the second important code used by the German navy. It was captured at the very start of the war in Australia, although it did not reach the Admiralty until the end of October. The German-Australian steamer Hobart was seized off Port Philip Heads near Melbourne on 11 August 1914. Hobart had not received news that war had broken out, and Captain J. T. Richardson and party claimed to be a quarantine inspection team. Hobart's crew was allowed to go about the ship but the captain was closely observed, until in the middle of the night he attempted to dispose of hidden papers. The HVB codebook was captured, which contained the code used by the German navy to communicate with its merchant ships and also within the High Seas Fleet. News of the capture was not passed to London until 9 September. A copy of the book was made and sent by the fastest available steamer, arriving end of October.

Capture of the VB (*Verkehrsbuch*) code book. On 30 November 1914 a British trawler recovered a safe from the sunken German destroyer S-119, in which was found the VB code book used by the Germans to communicate with naval attachés, embassies and warships overseas. The German destroyers S115, S117, S118, and S119 were all attacked and sunk in October 1914 by the Royal Navy, in the Battle of Texel Island in the North of Holland. The German ships were involved in a mine laying operation. The commander of S119 threw overboard all the ships secret papers in a metal safe. Both the German captain and the British who saw him do this believed the contents would have been destroyed. However on 30th of November 1914 possibly acting on orders from the admiralty a British trawler dragged up the safe which happened to contain the VB code book, the German flag officers code book.

All these three code-books were of great assistance to Room 40 in the early stages of the war. The Germans replaced code-books throughout the war but these captures gave Room 40 the insight in the way which the German code books were designed. These captures were instrumental in the future of code breaking operations at the admiralty during World War I.

The code-books were especially useful in the 1916 Battle of Jutland, where Admiral Jellicoe benefited from the decoded German signals. However, because they were never used to the full extent of their potential, Jellicoe lost many ships in this battle. In Churchill's words "Jellicoe was the only Admiral who could lose a war in an afternoon". On the slightly brighter side, the blockade of German ships was at least successful, but it came at a tremendous cost.

Code-breaking at room 40 was doing well, and when DNI Admiral Henry Oliver retired he was succeeded by Admiral Reginald Hall. Admiral Hall had a distinct squint when he got excited, so he acquired the name "blinker Hall". Admiral Hall increased the work of room 40 by giving greater priority to the interception of diplomatic cable-grams. The majority of these international submarine cables were owned by British companies and there was an existing act of Parliament that allowed the government to intercept them. NID 25 had great success at intercepting these diplomatic cables. When *CS Alert* cut many of the submarine cables linking Germany with the rest of the world, it unfortunately also cut off the United States with large parts of Europe. This became all very worthwhile in 1917 when code-breaker Nigel de Grey intercepted a diplomatic telegram that changed history. The Germans believed that their cable link to the USA, at this stage neutral, would be routed via Sweden. Little did they know, the link came via London. A message was sent from the German foreign minister Arthur Zimmerman to the German Embassy in Washington. This message was to be forwarded to Mexico, to encourage the Mexicans to side with Germany against the United States of America. The idea was to tie America up in a war on its own soil, and so prevent them from entering the European war. As an ally, the carrot for Mexico would be that Germany would assist the recovery of lost territories that had been taken by the USA as in Arizona, New Mexico, and Texas.

When Nigel de Grey realised the importance of this message, he knew that it was crucial to inform the president of the US, Woodrow Wilson. The problem was that if the Germans realised that we were intercepting their cables and breaking their code they would change their systems and we would be left out in the cold. So it was decided for the US to stage a break-in to the German Embassy in Washington and steal the decrypts. The idea was to make it look as if that was how we obtained the information about the Zimmerman telegram. When Woodrow Wilson received the Zimmerman proposal to Mexico he was furious about the Germans' interfering. It was shortly after this that the United States of America joined World War 1 as an ally to Britain. During the war, Room 40 became so successful that Foreign Secretary Lord Curzon decided that the code-breaking facility should be taken under the control of the government. In 1919 the section of the Admiralty known as NID25 merged with the army's code-breaking and intercept facility known as MI 1b, which was previously based at the war office in Whitehall. The foreign office arranged that the "Secret Intelligence Service "(MI6) would be the umbrella organisation for the code-breakers. The chief of SIS was Admiral Hugh Sinclair, and he was known as "C", which is still how the MI6 chief is referred to today. Commander Alistair Denniston was made operational head of the Government Code and Cipher School, the fancy new name for the British Governments code-breaking department. In the spring of 1926, after several office moves, it eventually settled at the MI6 Headquarters on floors three, four and five at 54 Broadway buildings, London SW1. A brass plate was mounted on the door of the building which stated "Minimax Fire Extinguisher Company", which of course was a complete fabrication and cover.

Between the wars

Between the wars there was very little code-breaking happening. The Government Code and Cipher School continued to operate with a reduced staff, many of its main players having returned to their old jobs, mainly in academia. The primary work of the GC&CS was now intercepting diplomatic cablegrams. It was also keeping an eye on the Trotskyist organisation called Comintern, which was committed to spreading communism across the globe. In England Comintern were trying to infiltrate the trade unions and newspapers, as well as setting up clandestine radio stations. A radio intercept station was set up by Harold Kenworthy with Metropolitan police at Denmark Hill in south London, from where signals were sent on to CG&GS at Broadway Buildings. In 1936 the GC&CS were also monitoring and deciphering signals from the Spanish Civil War. The Spanish were using the K type Enigma machine which was being used by the Spanish nationalist forces and also German and Italian forces supporting Franco.

On 30ᵗʰ January 1933 Adolf Hitler became Chancellor and took full command of Germany. He had named himself Führer, "Supreme leader". He and his National Socialist party (Nazis) were controlling Germany with a rod of iron and storm clouds were brewing as Hitler was brandishing his sabres at Europe. Britain initially tried appeasement but with Hitler's aggression Britain became aware of the possibility of another war. In September 1938, Prime Minister Neville Chamberlain made his last-ditch attempt to make peace with Hitler, known as the Munich Agreement. You may recall the film footage of Neville Chamberlain returning to London, stepping out of an aeroplane with a piece of paper flapping in the wind. Chamberlain stating the words "This piece of paper has my signature and Hitler's signature on it. It means peace for our time". Many people believed in their hearts that war was still in the offing. However, after a few weeks, with Hitler's shenanigans, it was obvious that the agreement was as shaky as the piece of paper it was written on. By March 1939 , with Hitler's aggressive action in Europe, Prime Minister Chamberlain signed the Anglo-Polish Military Pact which promised Poland that they would have the support and assistance of Britain should they be invaded by Germany.

Meanwhile, at Broadway Buildings, Admiral Sinclair and Commander Denniston realised that if Britain went to war with Germany again, London would more than likely be attacked by aerial bombing. It was decided that, like so many other government organisations, it was time to think about moving out of London to somewhere they could operate in a place of safety. Now with the possibility of the war approaching at an alarming rate the GC&CS initiated a big recruiting push. The personnel required to work at a code-breaking establishment had to be of a certain caliber: brilliant intellects, linguists and mathematicians. As Sinclair put it to Denniston, "Go the universities and search for the professor type." The hunting ground for these was to be the universities of Oxford and Cambridge. Therefore one of the considerations would be easy access to and from those university towns and of course good access to London by rail and road. Also a national competition was organised calling out for anyone who could complete a crossword puzzle in the Daily Telegraph within 12 minutes to come forward for special government work.

During mid 1938 in the Northern Buckinghamshire town of Bletchley, a Victorian country house became available. It was in a private country park consisting of 44 acres of landscaped gardens. The former home of Sir Herbert Samuel Leon, a very wealthy London stockbroker, it was now in the hands of a property developer, Captain Hubert Faulkner. Faulkner had plans to demolish the Victorian mansion, flatten the beautiful gardens for the sake of a housing estate. And in doing so build himself a large country house overlooking the lake, His plans had hardly started when he received a visit from a group of men from London purporting to be from "Captain Ridley's shooting party". In reality the group of men were from MI6 (SIS) and the Government Code & Cipher School, which included Admiral Sinclair, Commander Alistair Denniston and other senior officers. The party had already seen some unsuitable locations around the outskirts of London that never met the requirements.

The Mansion Bletchley Park

The Purchase

They now came to see Bletchley Park which appeared a good future possibility for a war station if the need were to arise. Bletchley Park had all the attributes required: good road links to London along the Watling Street; the mainline railway into London. It also had the main telephone trunk cable to the north-west of the country alongside the main road with a GPO repeater station just a mile away that could easily be used to divert hundreds of required telephone lines into the Bletchley Park which could become useful for extra communications also teleprinters. There was an added bonus of a cross-country railway line connecting the great university towns of Oxford and Cambridge, which came right through the centre of Bletchley. Captain Faulkner was made an offer he could not refuse.

Either the government would put a compulsory purchase order on the park, but this would take time but it would prevent Faulkner developing the site, or the estate could be requisitioned by the government, and then who knows when or whether that Faulkner would be paid. Or Faulkner could sell it to the government now.

Faulkner wanted £7,500 for the Bletchley Park mansion along with 44 acres of land. Admiral Sinclair took his cheque book out and said "I will offer you £6000 now, along with a contract to build temporary wooden huts". Captain

14

Faulkner agreed. So a deal was done, Admiral Sinclair paid Captain Faulkner £6000 for the Bletchley Park Mansion, along with the land which housed the beautiful gardens. A few staff moved in on a temporary basis at first to see if their systems could operate there effectively. Once they were happy that Bletchley Park could make a good headquarters for the code-breakers, Bletchley Park was all locked up and the executives moved back to London.

Bletchley Park was still top-secret, only a few members of "Captain Ridley's shooting party" were aware of the new facility. All staff were informed that should they receive a telegram stating that "Auntie Flo is feeling unwell" they should pack a suitcase and proceed to Euston station, and from there take a train to Bletchley. They were advised that they must not divulge to anyone where they were going, and that they would be met at Bletchley station by a representative of MI6. In August 1939, that message was indeed sent to all relevant staff working at Broadway buildings. When they arrived at Bletchley Park, they were interviewed by the security officers and had to sign the Official Secrets Act, if they had not already done so. They were then reminded not to murmur a word of where they were to be working, or what they were doing, to a single soul - including family, friends, and even colleagues - especially in the staff canteen or at the railway station. They were told very clearly that if any of this was disobeyed, it would be a treasonable offence and the penalty would be most severe. That is why even today many veterans who worked at Bletchley Park during the war are unhappy or uneasy to talk of their experiences. 138 staff initially moved into Bletchley Park in August 1939 from the Government Code & Cipher School. The code-breakers were not alone, part of their umbrella organisation moved in with them, namely MI6 including section VIII the Communications department, loosely known as the Diplomatic Wireless Service. It was their job to send messages to our agents and embassies all over the world. Our agents were normally based at the British passport offices at the British embassies. It must be noted here that we call our agents "agents" and foreign agents are known as "spies". The original radio station at Bletchley Park was located in a converted water tower on the roof of the mansion house, a further radio room was within Hut 1.

All MI6 radio stations were given numbers; Bletchley Park was allocated number 10. The numbers were listed and quoted in Roman numerals, so

Bletchley Park became known as Station X, which is nothing more sinister than radio station number 10 in the diplomatic wireless service.

The day war broke out
Virtually everyone in the country was listening to their wireless set at 11am on Sunday 3rd September 1939.

"This is the BBC National service," said the announcer. "We now take you to 10 Downing Street for a message from the Prime Minister." After a short silence the voice of Prime Minister Neville Chamberlain was heard:

"I am speaking to you from the Cabinet Room at 10 Downing Street. This morning, the British ambassador in Berlin handed the German government a final note stating that, unless we heard from them by 11 o'clock to say that they were prepared at once to withdraw their troops from Poland, a state of war would exist between us. I have to tell you now that no such undertaking has been received, and that consequently this country is at war with Germany."

And so Station X became a fully operational war station. To staff, the station would always be known as "BP". It was soon realised that the array of aerials on the roof of the mansion was not only visible to enemy reconnaissance aircraft, but that their transmissions could be detected and location pinpointed by enemy direction-finding equipment. So in November 1939, the aerials were removed from Bletchley Park and the whole of MI6 section VIII moved 4½ miles west, to the village of Whaddon Bucks and into another one of these country houses, Whaddon Hall. The establishment became known as the Special Communications Unit 1 (SCU1). During World War II this was the main radio station for all MI6 transmissions, especially for dissemination of the decrypted signals from Bletchley Park, which were sent to overseas mobile receiving stations known as SLUs (special liaison units). The SLUs would deliver the top secret information called Ultra to the commanders in the theatre of war. Initially, different rooms at Bletchley Park's Victorian mansion house were used for deciphering messages from German army, air force or naval signals.

How the Park worked

In World War 1 the Germans used code-books to change their military signals into an unreadable state. In the Second World War, they used cipher machines to encrypt their signals. In simple terms the difference between code and a cipher is that the code-book is one method whereby you would look up a word in a list, then change it to the corresponding word in an adjacent list, which could only be retrieved if you were in possession of the said code book. A cipher is different, it changes the construction of the word by substituting the letters in the word for other letters. This would change a plain word, or plain text, into cipher-text or maybe you might call it gobbledygook. The cipher-text would be completely unreadable. The authorised receiving agent would have to apply the same method of encryption in reverse to decrypt the text back to the original plain text format and thus making it readable.

Enigma

In World War II the Germans used several different types of machine to change their military messages into an unreadable format. The most popular and widely used was the Enigma machine. It was not a new invention. The Enigma machine was originally invented in 1919 as a commercial machine. There were many different versions available then. In 1926 the model M3 was on trial with the *Reichswehr* (name of the German military between 1919 and 1935 meaning Defence Force), and eventually became responsible for the majority of enciphered enemy signals. A message would be written out in plain German, this was entered letter by letter into the Enigma machine. Then the message would travel via a series of electrical connections and mechanical scrambler wheels to finally become enciphered. The message text would appear one letter at a time onto a lamp indicator board. By the time the *Wehrmacht* became the military power of Germany from October 1935, operative Enigma machines numbered tens of thousands. By 1944 it is said that the German military possessed in excess of 80,000 Enigma machines and they were in use across the Axis powers on almost 200 communication networks.

Enigma M3
With kind permission Bletchley Park Trust

Y-stations

For the German military to send a message from one unit to another, the sending station would type the German plain text into the Enigma machine, and this encrypted message was then sent by the radio operator, using standard International Morse code. The radio signals were picked up by our wireless intercept stations, known as Y-stations. The stations were mainly along the south and east coasts of Britain, with a few also situated inland.

They were operated by the ladies of the armed services: the Wrens (navy), WAFFS (air force), and the ATS (army). As we knew the radio frequencies being used by the various sections of the German military it was normal practice for our Wrens to intercept *"Kriegsmarine"* naval signals, our WAFFS to intercept *"Luftwaffe"* air force signals and the ATS to intercept *"Heer"* signals from the German army. The Y-station staff were given a radio set and told which German radio frequencies to monitor. Some of the signals were very weak, coming right across war-torn Europe, but accuracy was absolutely paramount, as a single incorrect letter could inhibit a code-breakers work. There were other Y-stations duplicating the same radio frequencies so the messages could be eventually compared for accuracy.

Once a message was complete it would be packaged up and sent to Bletchley Park. In the early part of the war, this was mainly achieved by many dispatch riders travelling at high speeds across the length and breadth of the country. All sign posts had been removed for security reasons and to travel at night you had very limited head lamps owing to the blackout conditions and in all weathers. Many of these dispatch riders were women, who delivered the signals urgently to Bletchley Park. Sometimes Bletchley Park received over forty dispatch riders within a 24-hour day. Later on in the war over two hundred teleprinters were installed at Bletchley Park to connect up with the Y-stations.

Staff at Bletchley Park

When Bletchley Park first became operational in August 1939, there was 138 staff. By 1944, over 10,000 people were working there and running outstations at Stanmore and Eastcote in Middlesex. There were also more distant outstations in India and Egypt. 85% of Bletchley staff was in the military. There was no marching up and down (square bashing), no saluting, it was just all very informal. 75% of the military staff were ladies of the women's Royal Naval Service known as the "Wrens" (WRNS). Many of the Wrens joined the service probably to be near the coast, maybe with the occasional sunshine there might be the possibility of a visit to the beach.

The Wrens were to be stationed at *HMS Pembroke 5*, which was not a ship but another name for Bletchley Park, about as far from the sea as it's possible to be in Britain! Staff at Bletchley worked a shift system: from 08:00 hours to 16:00 hours; 16:00 hours to midnight; and midnight to 8 in the morning. Instead of living on the site, staff was all billeted out to hotels guesthouses, bed-and-breakfast, and digs, depending on their status of course. Some billets were quite some distance away in Northamptonshire, Bedfordshire and Oxfordshire. Transport was provided in the form of buses and coaches but mainly from army trucks with wooden plank seats. This was all arranged by the transport manager who was the only member of staff that lived on site, along with his family. Most staff travelled to and from these billets by bicycle. If you visit Bletchley Park today, you will see many bike sheds with old bicycle in them at various locations as a reminder of this common mode of transport.

The Huts and blocks

With the many thousands of staff at Bletchley Park huts were quickly built as a temporary solution for working and leisure, as well as some religious services. Those temporary huts built in 1940 are still at Bletchley Park today and form part of the museum's displays. Working huts were named in pairs: Hut 3 and Hut 6 worked together, as did Hut 4 and Hut 8.

As personnel numbers increased, staff moved to permanent brick buildings known as blocks. The departments took their hut numbers with them and the original huts were then renumbered this was so you were unable to identify what each hut actually did, you only know if you needed to know, (a need to know basis). Hut 6, headed by Gordon Welchman and assisted by his number two Stuart Milner Barry, was responsible for breaking the codes of the German army (*Heer*) and German air force (*Luftwaffe*). Once the code was broken and the German text was extracted from gobbledygook, the code-breakers in Hut 6 would send the raw text to Hut 3 for translation and analysis. There it would be decided how urgent signals were.

We must remember that these messages were not written in standard German, they were written in barrack-room slang and technical data. Representatives of the army and air force worked in Hut 3 to assist in analysing the information. Each operation had its commander in charge who would collate everything gathered and move it along. These signals were sent by teleprinter or radio, enciphered onto our code system: TYPEX. The Germans never broke into our TYPEX system, which is a miracle as its design and operating system were based on the German Enigma machine. Signals for the RAF were sent by teleprinter down to the head of fighter command at Bentley Priory north of London. If they were for the Army they would be sent direct to the commanders in the theatre of war via the radio station at Whaddon Hall. Winston Churchill was very concerned that the enemy should not realise that their signals had been broken. He was also very concerned that no one at Whitehall should find out that the information coming out of Bletchley was coming from broken German codes. Therefore, in the early days of Bletchley Park, the decrypted messages were disguised as agent reports, which were compiled by the MI6 offices that were housed on the first floor of the Bletchley park mansion. The "agent reports" would then be passed to Whitehall in special pink covers called "Pimpernels", purporting to come from the (non-existent) Agent Boniface.

British Typex Cipher Machine
With kind permission Bletchley Park Trust

Traffic analysis

This is another important function of Bletchley Park that was set out by Gordon Welchman and comander Ellingwoth of the Army Y-station originally at Chatham in Kent and later moved to Beau Manor Leicestershire. When a Y-Station would receive a signal our direction finding teams would work out where the signal was coming from using high frequency direction-finding equipment (HF/DF commonly called *huf-duf*). A department at Bletchley Park known as Fusion would look at and analyse these reports. By identifying call-signs you could accuracy trace the movements of mobile enemy forces. This information once again would be passed on to our commanders.

Hut 8 and Hut 4: Naval code-breaking

Hut 8 was the naval code-breaking Hut. It was headed by Alan Turing, and second-in-command was Hugh Alexander. Frank Burch, head of naval section, gave Alan Turing the job, and told him "you may find naval Enigma impossible to break." Turing replied, "That's good, I like impossible tasks!" The reason for this was that naval Enigma was far more complex than the army and airforce

21

versions. To start with they had to choose three rotors out of a box of eight as per their daily setting instructions. When a ship or enemy submarine (U-boat) would send a radio signal, they were very aware that that signal could give their position away very quickly as the British were using very efficient direction-finding equipment (HF/DF). So to keep transmissions as short as possible, the German navy would use a shortened version of standard phrases, as per the instruction of a "short signal code-book". Then the coded message was typed into the Enigma machine and sent by radio in Morse code. This type of message had then become "super enciphered". This gave Alan Turing a real headache. When he took on his assistant Hugh Alexander, Turing said "I understand that you play chess" "Yes," Alexander replied, "I am the 1938 British chess champion." To which, Turing remarked "Have I got a chess problem for you!" The Hut 8 team did break naval Enigma throughout the war but there were some massive gaps. Once the plaintext message had been extracted from the cipher text, the information was passed to Hut 4 for translation and analysis. The signals were then sent down to the Admiralty in London by teleprinter. They were received at the operational intelligence centre (OIC), located deep under Horse Guards Parade known as the Citadel. Winston Churchill required all naval Enigma messages to be sent directly to him in a locked box. I doubt very much if he got all of them. There was probably a concern that Churchill had a reputation with interfering with operations. You can still see the part of the citadel on the west flank of the Old Admiralty buildings, the massive reinforced bomb proof concrete edifice which was once formed the main entrance. The admirals in charge of these control rooms would once again analyse the signals assess their urgency and signal the fleet directly.

Ultra

All decrypted messages that left Bletchley Park were called Ultra. Winston Churchill said that the work of Bletchley Park was not just top-secret, but was Ultra -top secret. The word Ultra became adopted for all information leaving Bletchley Park. The commanders were not informed whether the messages came from Bletchley Park or from the broken Enigma code; all they needed to know was that it was very reliable information. To use Ultra you had to have a second source of information to prevent the enemy from learning that their codes were being broken. If your enemy suspected that their codes were being compromised they would simply change them, and you would be back to square one. If, for example, a commander of operations were to receive an Ultra-signal to say that there was a fleet of enemy ships passing by within the next few hours, he would need a suitable dummy source for that information. In order to prevent those enemy ships believing that the information was attained from their codes a spotter plane could be sent up, not necessarily to locate the ships but to get close enough that the enemy would believe that was how they became discovered. This became a very dangerous operation as many of the spotter planes were shot down. Another method that was used was to put an insertion into a German newspaper after the event in a simple code that could be easily broken, thanking one of our agents for information which had led us to achieve some military advantage. Of course these agents, or spies, were a complete fabrication. We gave some of them pay rises along with promotion, even though they had never even existed. If you ever read any of Winston Churchill's accounts of World War II he will never mention the words ultra, Enigma or even Bletchley Park. If he needed to cover the question of any intelligence he would say it came from "most secret sources" or from his personal spy Boniface. The agent Boniface was also a complete invention of Winston Churchill's imagination.

Polish connection

In our journey to Station X, we must talk about the Polish connection within the Enigma code-breaking. We will cover this in the chapter called "So, who broke the Enigma code anyway?" The Author, who is also a volunteer guide at Bletchley Park, is frequently asked by visitors if Bletchley Park was ever bombed in the war. The Germans never knew of the existence or whereabouts of Bletchley Park, if they did know they would certainly have attacked it and flattened it. But there was one incident which occurred in November 1940 when a lone German bomber approached Bletchley Park from the South. We believe it was probably part of a much larger raid and that this one pilot had been separated from the main body of the raiders, and in starting to head back to Germany he decided to dispose of his bombs. It is suspected that he would have aimed at the large railway junction and sidings at Bletchley station. However, this German pilot had all his sights wrong and dropped a stick of six bombs, four of which landed in a wooded area just south of the Park, in a clump of trees.

It has been said that the blast blew the naval intelligence hut 4 off its foundations. It has also been said that it was picked up and put back into its original position by Royal Naval engineers working on site, while people were still working inside it. Like so many other stories surrounding Bletchley Park, there is no proof that this happened; Hut 4 is 145 foot long by 30 foot wide. Another bomb did fall on a former school and partly demolished the building. It was being used by Bletchley Park for administration, but fortunately there were no casualties. The final bomb fell in the stable yard just north of the mansion house. It has been said that it fell straight through into an underground water tank, and it never exploded. It was defused on site since they could not remove it. Sources suggest that it is still there today.

Stable yard

In the stable yard there is a row of three cottages that date back to the Leon family which accommodated their chauffeurs and their head gardeners during the turn of the twentieth century. During the Second World War, cottage number two is where the transport manager Mr. Budd and his family lived. He was responsible for organising the vehicles for taking staff, of which there were many, to-and-from the more distant billets. On the three shift turnarounds, transport had to be available on time. These days number three cottage is probably the most historically-important building on site. This is where, in January 1940, the Enigma code was broken for the first time in Britain. This was achieved by a team of code-breakers led by Alfred Dillwyn Knox, known then as "Dilly" Knox. The team also consisted of John Jefferies, Peter Twin, mathematician Margaret Rock; 28 year-old Alan Turing; and a brilliant 19 year-old linguist by the name of Mavis Lever. Mavis, who passed away in 2013, left some very good stories about the goings-on in number three cottage, in a book called "Dilly". Also in this tiny cottage, a further seven Wrens worked. The head-of-section Knox loved working with women, but Mavis reported that he always behaved himself. He spent more time looking for his pipe tobacco and his glasses than anything else. Dilly Knox was a World War 1 veteran code-breaker from the Admiralty Room 40 days. He was an Egyptologist by profession but was now a very eccentric, brilliant code-breaker. But the question is: where did he get the Enigma machine from? This will be revealed in the chapter about the Polish code-breakers. Outside cottage number three is a memorial to three brilliant Polish mathematicians and the Polish code-breakers from the cipher bureau in Warsaw in the 1930s.

War efforts

In early 1940, Hitler had planned to invade Britain. He called it Operation Sea-lion as this was going to be a seaborne invasion of the south coast. To implement this he knew that the RAF had to be obliterated. He ordered Herman Goering, the commander of the *Luftwaffe*, the German air force, to entice the whole RAF into the sky in great numbers. The *Luftwaffe*, in excess of four times larger than the RAF, would easily exterminate them. All these signals were intercepted, decoded, translated and then sent immediately to Chief Air Marshall Hugh Dowding, the head of fighter command at Bently Priory near Stanmore, north of London. Dowding, being privy to Ultra, received the signals and decided not to send great numbers of aircraft into the sky. He sent the "few", the Spitfires and the hurricanes to cause mayhem and confusion for Herman Goering and the *Luftwaffe*. This period of time was known as the Battle of Britain. Our small groups of brave pilots battled day after day with the *Luftwaffe*. The intelligence was coming from combined information Ultra and radar also the Observer Corps. But no matter how many times the mighty *Luftwaffe* tried to attack Britain, we sent them back with their tails between their legs. We did lose many aircraft, airfields and personnel but due to brave airmen and accurate signals intelligence such as Ultra we managed to beat them off. The main attack in the Battle of Britain the Germans called Eagle Day *(Adlertag)*, on the 13th August 1940, which was another unmitigated disaster for the *Luftwaffe*. It is possible that due to the frustrations we caused Herman Goering in not being able to remove the RAF, our British cities received an even more intense pounding in the Blitz. It was now becoming too late in the year for Adolf Hitler's plan for a seaborne invasion. It was now September with the winter weather was drawing in, and this type of operation would have not worked. Hitler was now turning his sights east towards the Soviet Union.

North Africa

If you are fighting a war in the desert you will be very dependent on your supply lines. When and where are your ammunition, food, water and replacements for the damaged equipment coming from? In North Africa in 1941 Italian, then later German, forces were fighting to try to get through and overrun Egypt. General Archibald Wavell, Field Marshal Claude Auchinleck, and then Field Marshal Bernard Montgomery were defending the position. The British commanders were privy to Ultra, and they would have intercepted German signals delivered to them by special liaison units (SLUs). The information not only gave away many of the German positions of battle but more importantly, the locations of Field Marshal Erwin Rommel's supply lines. We knew from Ultra that the Italians were delivering supplies to certain North African ports. We also knew of when they would arrive, and this information would be seen by the RAF and the Royal Navy who would attack Rommel's supply ships. The desired effect worked, and it would prove devastating to Rommel's plan of action. This was especially revalent to the outcome of the second Battle of El Alamein. Rommel was starved of supplies due to Allied action which was a direct result of the ultra emanating from Bletchley Park.

Mattapan

Previously in this chapter we spoke of a lady linguist who worked with Dilly Knox's team at number three cottage at Bletchley Park. Her name was Mavis Lever. One evening, she was working with some decrypted Italian messages. Mavis was translating what turned out to be Italian naval Battle Plans. It was recognised that many Italian warships were gathering to attack the British naval base at Crete. In part of the decrypted message Mavis noticed the characters X-3. X-3 = (X minus 3) the letter X on a battle plan refers to the word day so X-3 would signify that something big was going to happen in three days time; The allies use the letter "D" for the same principle. The day of the battle is always called D Day, so D+1 would mean the second day of the battle etc. Once this was discovered Bletchley Park immediately informed the Admiralty who sent an urgent signal to Admiral Andrew Cunningham the commander in chief of the Eastern Mediterranean fleet. Cunningham was on his flag ship *HMS Warspite* in the port of Alexandria. When Cunningham received the signal he realised he had to act very carefully. He knew that any move he made would get back to the Italians immediately, as Alexandria was a hotbed of spies. Cunningham being a cool kind of guy with his best white crisp naval uniform, made sure that everyone saw him leave the port to supposedly play golf. As a double bluff, he also arranged to go to a non-existent dinner party, and have some dummy suitcases delivered to a local hotel for an overnight stay. But as night fell, he crept back to his ship and took his whole fleet out in total darkness. They caught up with the Italian Navy, caught them by surprise and gave them the biggest bashing they had ever had. Admiral Cunningham virtually wrecked the majority of the Italian Navy in one swoop. One Italian battleship heavily damaged *Vittorio Veneto;* The British also sank three heavy cruisers and two destroyers; killed over 2,300; and took 1,015 POWs. Winston Churchill commented that it was the biggest battle since Jutland in 1916 and the biggest victory since the Battle of Trafalgar in 1805. We never had a problem with the Italian Navy after that incident; they never again dared to come anywhere close to the Royal Navy. It happened in the days when we urgently needed victories and this was a big one. All because a young 19 year old linguist working in a Victorian cottage in Buckinghamshire recognised the situation and immediately passed it on to her superiors. Later in the war when Admiral Andrew Cunningham became first Sea Lord he came to Bletchley Park and thanked the girls personally for their part they played in the battle of Cape Mattapan.

Action this day

Prime Minister Winston Churchill was very impressed with his most secret source of information. He came to Bletchley Park 6th September 1941 to see for himself how the staff operated. He stood on a large stone outside the front of the Mansion house and spoke to the staff. He told them that they were "the geese that laid the golden eggs and never cackled" as every one of the staff was sworn to complete secrecy. The only thing they could tell their inquisitive landladies and landlords was that Bletchley Park was the control station for London's air defence. That was the cover story, that and nothing more. Some locals thought that the strange characters going in and out of Bletchley Park in large numbers every day must mean it's some kind of lunatic asylum. Intact the locals would threaten their naughty children that if they did not behave they would be sent into Bletchley Park by men in white coats.

In spite of all the successes that Bletchley was having, things were not going well at all. The possibilities of breaking a daily key on the Enigma machine on one communications network was 159 million million million-to-one. The key changed every night at zero hour GMT. That meant that all the settings on the Enigma machine changed every night. Plus, there were almost two hundred networks. The German military had code-books for every theatre of war including the SS, *Luftwaffe*, railways, dockyards; even the Italians were given Enigma system and later in the war the Japanese had the version "T" of the Enigma machine. Thousands of messages were coming in every day from the wireless intercept stations and the staff did not have the resources to complete the work. Frustration reigned. To this end, Alan Turing invented a machine with the assistance of Gordon Welchman, head of Hut 6, and Harold "Doc" Keen of the British Tabulating Machine Company of Letchworth Hertfordshire. It was called the Bombe machine, which had nothing to do with high explosives and was an unfortunate name for a machine for use in the war. Alan Turing said "159 million million million-to-one was a needle in a haystack." He added, "The best way to find a needle in a haystack is to remove the hay."

The Bombe machine worked out the day's Enigma settings by eliminating most of the unfeasible options this reduced that massive figure to a mere handful of 4.6 million. They already had several Bombe machines on test, but with the vast amount of work coming in from the Y-stations, they needed hundreds of these machines to clear the work. However, there was a considerable cost, not only of production, but Wrens were needed to operate them and RAF technicians to keep them serviced. The team approached the operational head of Bletchley Park, Commander Denniston, but he could not ask for any more money. Denniston was in a Catch-22 situation. In order to ask for further funding, he needed to approach the Foreign Office, since they pulled the purse strings of Bletchley Park, but being sworn to secrecy he could not say what the money was to be used for, so the money was not forthcoming. This frustrated the code-breakers, as they knew that unbroken codes equated to lost lives especially in the battle of the Atlantic, so they decided to write a letter direct to Winston Churchill. The letter was composed by Alan Turing, his deputy Hugh Alexander, the head of hut 6 Gordon Welchman, and his deputy Stuart Milner

Barry. The letter was three pages long, with the gist as follows: They explained to Churchill how the majority of the work coming from the wireless intercept stations was left on the cutting-room floor.

Whilst they were aware that their work saved lives, they never had the resources to deal with everything that came in from the wireless intercept stations. They also advised him that they had done all they could to try and raise funds for the purchase and production of hundreds of Bombe machines. They added that they had no intention to upstage, Edward Travis the deputy head of Bletchley Park, who they said tried his best to get funding. They decided to deliver this letter by hand, and that Stuart Milner Barry would take it to 10 Downing Street himself. In those days you could walk along Downing Street and knock on the door. Nowadays, security measures mean that you can't get anywhere near there.

Milner Barry went to London and walked down Downing Street, knocked on the door of number 10 and asked to see the Prime Minister on urgent national security business. He was asked where he came from, but of course Milner Barry was not allowed to murmur the word Bletchley Park to anyone who was not authorised. He was told that the best outcome would be that his letter was delivered to the Prime Minister's private secretary, Brigadier Harvie-Walker. Milner Barry thought that no one would ever see it again, since the civil service had a reputation for inefficiency, especially in Whitehall. But Winston Churchill did see that letter. He read it, and was very concerned as Churchill was a great supporter of Bletchley Park which produced his information "Boniface", also known as Ultra. He stamped the wording across the top "ACTION THIS DAY: then wrote the following memo "Make sure they have all they want on extreme priority and report to me when this has been done signed WSC." That letter was then handed to his chief of staff General Ismay (Hastings Lionel "Pug" Ismay) and funds started rolling into Bletchley Park almost immediately. The Bombe machines were built. We do not know if it was a result of this letter, but Commander Alistair Denniston the head of Bletchley Park was then soon replaced by his deputy Commander Edward Travis, a much tougher man, which was probably what was needed to take charge of this now massive organisation. But we must give credit to Cmdr Alistair Denniston who had the foresight to acquire the right kind of personnel "the professor type" from the universities of Oxford and Cambridge and set up the operational structure of Bletchley Park.

Denniston was moved to work at Berkeley Street, London, in charge of the diplomatic code-breaking section, which he believed was a demotion and he was always very bitter over this move. There is little doubt that Commander Alexander (Alastair) Guthrie Denniston CMG CBE RNVR was the architect of the GC&CS at Bletchley Park.

Bombe Machines
© Crown. Reproduced by kind permission, Director, GCHQ

With kind permission Bletchley Park Bombe Rebuild Project

U Boats and the Battle of the Atlantic

On 5th October 1943, Admiral Andrew Cunningham, 1st Sea Lord, said "It takes three years to build a battleship; it takes three hundred years to build a tradition." The Navy Royal as it was known was formed in Tudor times initially by King Henry VIII. The Royal Navy was properly formed later, hence Cunningham's words of three hundred years of tradition. In 1939, prior to World War II the Royal Navy was still the largest naval force in the world, even after the Washington and London naval treaties, which attempted to stem a global naval arms race. Let us initially look at the types of ships that were in use during World War II

The battleship: This was the largest most heavily-armoured ship. An example would be *HMS King George V,* which was commissioned in 1940. Weighing 42,200 tons, heavily-armoured, and with a speed of twenty-eight knots. The main cannons were mounted on revolving turrets that could fire a 360mm shell, weighing almost a ton, approximately eighteen miles. *HMS King George V* had ten of these cannons, making her a battleship and an extremely powerful weapon.

The cruiser: For example, *HMS Belfast 1938.* At 11,550 tons this had twelve 102mm turreted guns and could sail at thirty-two knots. Being lighter and less well-armoured, the cruiser was a quick ship and good for chasing U-boats also escorting heavier battleships. The HMS Belfast is now owned by the Imperial War Museum and if you're on the south-side of Tower Bridge, opposite the Tower of London, you can visit it in her current home on the River Thames.

The destroyer: Like *HMS Cavalier 1944,* which had a speed of thirty-seven knots and weighed 1,710 tons. With three 114mm cannons, destroyers destroy things, especially U-boats. They were heavily-armed and fast, and could also act as an escort for cruisers.

The Corvette: (Flower Class) under one thousand tons. These were built as escort vessels for merchant convoys. With a speed of sixteen knots, and a range of 3,500 miles, this small, versatile but very uncomfortable ship was used by several different navies: The United States navy, the Royal Canadian navy and the Royal Navy. Many of the crew were permanently seasick, as the buoyancy of this ship was problematic at best. Water leaked into accommodation and food preparation areas (the galley). Normally commanded by ex-merchant seamen, these small ships were used for convoy protection and were very successful. They were also successful at locating and chasing U-boats, since they were armed with depth charges and other weapons: 1 x 102mm BL Mk.IX single gun; two Vickers twin machine guns; two twin Lewis machine guns; two Mk.II depth charge throwers; and two depth charge rails with forty depth charges. Other types of Royal Naval ships included aircraft carriers, submarines mine layers and minesweepers.

Warship Weaponry

A warship's main turrets hold the big guns on the front and rear of many ships. There were also depth charges, which were an anti-U-boat weapon consisting of large drums of highly explosive material, normally Torpex. The detonator fires at a predetermined depth, and a wax insert gives way under a certain pressure of water, depending on the required depth. Unlike the shell or a bomb there is no steel casing to explode and splinter, the depth charge relies on a shockwave from the pressure of water at the point of detonation. If the detonation is close enough, the pressure will cause up to sixteen massive shock waves, which may cause fatigue on the U-boat's hull, weakening the infrastructure, damaging internal equipment and maybe even smashing a hole into its side. Depth charges are normally launched by a spring-loaded firing mechanism from one of the sides of a ship, or rolled off the back as it sails over the top of the U-boat. You must be travelling at a fair rate of knots to clear the depth charge when it explodes otherwise you could well blow yourself up! Also employed was a battery of twenty-four high-explosive bombs launched from a matrix-type rack, known as "Hedgehog", which would detonate on contact with the U-boat. With good aim, this proved a very effective weapon. There was a forward-facing weapon, known as "Squid", used for chasing U-boats. The Squid had three forward-facing firing tubes for firing missiles over the front of your ship. Once again, you must judge your aim correctly or you could shoot yourself down.

ASDIC (Allied Submarine Detection Information Committee), better known also as Sonar, was originally invented in 1917 but not put into full use until 1939, and its reliability improved over the war years. In the early days of the war, it could be said that too much reliance was given to sonar, with too little training for the operators. The apparatus transmits very high-frequency sound waves which upon contact with a metal object, reflects back to the receiver with the classic "ping". The nearer the object, the louder and closer together the pinging sound is heard. Later versions of ASDIC had a cathode ray tube that could indicate the three-dimensional position of the U-boat.

Germany did not have a plan to attack the Royal Navy, but instead had a plan to obliterate British merchant shipping fleets and starve Britain into submission. However, in doing this, if they encountered Royal Navy ships they had orders to engage them. In the First World War, U-boats successfully attacked and sank thousands of tonnes of our merchant shipping. Now, thirty years later they were doing it all over again. As in the First World War U-boats were deadly weapons, armed with torpedoes. A torpedo is a bomb fired from the U-boat through a chamber of compressed air. Once fired into the sea, it is driven by a reservoir of compressed air. Later versions of torpedoes were driven by battery power, which drove a gyro stabiliser and a propeller. The warhead contained high explosive and a contact detonator. Later torpedoes in World War II benefited from magnetic detonators and homing devices but these were not always very successful. The danger of the U-boats' was highlighted early in World War 1 with the sinking of the Cunard ship *RMS Lusitania*, which had a regular run between New York and Liverpool. This voyage was advertised in most American newspapers, but in May 1915 the German Imperial Embassy placed an advert directly underneath the *Lusitania's* advert, stating that "should the *RMS Lusitania* sail into a war zone or enemy waters it will become a target and will be liable for destruction." On 15th May 1915, *U-20* attacked, and *RMS Lusitania* sank within eighteen minutes, with a loss of 1,198 lives.

After Germany's defeat in the First World War, the U-boat fleets were scuttled or scrapped. The Treaty of Versailles was set out by many countries and was signed on 18th June 1919. The three main players were the United States, Britain and France, and it was principally to prevent Germany going to war again. The effect was to limit the armaments, so as to allow Germany to only have a defensive role. There were many conditions laid out in the treaty but the main features were: a limitation of 100,000 army personnel; any new capital warship i.e. battleship would be limited to an unladen weight of 40,000 tons; no U-boats were allowed to be built or used; no air force was to be formed; and reparations were to be made to repay the cost of the war. The amount was eventually agreed was 132 billion gold marks.

The idea of the treaty was to allow Germany enough military personnel and machinery to defend itself but not to become an aggressor. However, loopholes in articles 188 to 191 allowed the Germans to maintain the technology for building their U-boats. It also allowed the retention of designers and other technical staff. The loophole also allowed Germany to build U-boats in other countries such as Argentina, Sweden, and Italy. During the 1920s, as a result of the treaty of Versailles, Germany was going broke. Inflation was out of control, money became worthless, and people were feeling humiliated. Germany was in a complete and utter depression. So there was no surprise that a certain man who the Germans believed would be their *diamond geezer* came along and could make people believe that he could solve all of their problems if they supported and voted for him (*future voters beware*).

Blaming all of Germany's problems on the communists and the Jews, his political party was called "The National Socialist German Workers' Party *Nationalsozialistische Deutsche Arbeiterpartei*" abbreviated to (NSDAP), or Nazi Party. On the 30th January 1933, the National Socialist party gained power in Germany, led by Adolf Hitler who immediately disregarded the treaty of Versailles. He maintained that the treaty was a stab in the back for Germany and therefore completely ignored its terms and very soon implemented a plan for rearmament.

The head of the German Navy, Grand Admiral Erich Raeder, knew that the German Navy could never compete in a head-to-head battle with the Royal Navy. From their past knowledge from the First World War. The Germans knew that the best way to defeat the British would be to attack our trading routes using U-boats. It was also decided to construct two massive battleships the first part of a much larger rebuilding process known as "plan Z", this would potentially increase the size of the German surface fleet that could eventually rule the seas. In 1936, construction started on the 45,000 ton ship *Bismarck*, and soon after that, her sister ship *Tirpitz*.

Admiral Karl Doenitz was a World War 1 ex-submariner who made it through the ranks to become commander of the U-boats. He believed that control of the sea could be taken with just three-hundred U-boats, which would be far cheaper and more effective than using huge battleships. On 3rd September 1939, after a period of Nazi Germany's complete disregard for its neighbours' borders, Britain's Prime Minister Neville Chamberlain advised the nation that once again Britain was at war with Germany.

Admiral Doenitz had his U-boats ready, but he only had fifty-seven available, and some of these were Italian which were designed for the Mediterranean and were not suitable for use in the use in the North Atlantic. Nevertheless, on the first day of war, the German U-boat *U-30* commanded by Kapitan Fritz Julius Lemp, spotted the passenger ship *SS Athenia*. This ship was of the Donaldson Atlantic Line, its 1,103 passengers included Jewish refugees escaping the Nazis, as well as Canadians, US citizens and seventy-two UK subjects, as well as 315 crew.

The *SS Athenia* was en route from Glasgow to Montréal via Liverpool and Belfast. She left Liverpool at 13:00 hrs on 2nd September. On the evening of 3rd September 1939, her position was sixty nautical miles (110 km) south of Rockall, and two-hundred nautical miles (370 km) northwest of Inishtrahull, Ireland. The 13,500 ton ship was soon in the periscope sights of Fritz Julius Lemp. He then fired two torpedoes which struck the *Athenia* and it started to sink. Most of the passengers were returning back to the United States to escape the war. At 2210, a Mayday message was received by the ship-to-shore Marconi-gram service: "SOS from steam ship *Athenia*. Position 56° 44'N, 14° 05'W. Torpedoed. 1400 passengers. Some still on board. Sinking fast" SS *Athenia* finally sank at 10:40 the following morning, with the loss of 117 lives. The Germans immediately sent conflicting reports to the world's media, along the lines of "it was not us, it must have been the British", insinuating that the British did it to try and encourage the USA to enter the war. Then came another statement, claiming that *U-30* had mistaken the passenger ship as a troopship, known as a Q-ship or an armed merchant cruiser. Therefore, it was a legitimate target. Kapitan Lemp should have been court-marshalled for his error but instead he was quietly awarded the Iron Cross.

U-boat. U 36 Type VIIA
Reproduced by kind permission of the Bundesarchiv Germany

Winston Churchill believed that ASDIC sonar would be the pinnacle of U-boat detection. So it was ordered that all Royal Naval ships patrolling the Western approaches should be equipped with this device. However, the operating crews were denied proper training and didn't fully understand how to read the indicator screens. This issue had come to a head on 17th December 1939 when the aircraft carrier *HMS Courageous* was used in an anti-U-boat detection patrol. The 24,000 ton warship was converted to an aircraft carrier in 1924, with a complement of 1,217 crew and forty-eight aircraft. When it came into the sights of *U-20*, commanded by Kapitan Lieutenant Schuhart, the aircraft carrier was about to meet its maker. Schuhart fired three torpedoes, *HMS Courageous* rolled over and sank within twenty minutes with the loss of 119 crew. Her last Position 50.10N, 14.45W. West of Ireland. Kapitan Lieutenant Schuhart also received an Iron Cross for this action. Also in the vicinity was the aircraft carrier *HMS Ark Royal* which was hastily removed from this area.

Scapa Flow

The Orkney Islands had been a base and safe haven for Royal Naval ships for hundreds of years. An early warning to what was in store may well have been the successful intrusion in World War 1 by a German U-boat. This may have well been long-forgotten. This natural harbour protected by a small group of islands called Scapa Flow is where the Royal Navy believed their ships would be safe from attack. At the end of World War 1 many German ships were brought to the Scapa Flow to be possibly used by the Royal Navy. The defeated

German crews sailed through the narrow channels. They then scuttled all of their ships in defiance, blocking many of the entrances and exits to the British naval base. The Germans had felt so humiliated by the defeat in World War I that they wanted a chance to get revenge. As a precaution, the Royal Navy used some of the old scuttled World War 1 German ships to blockade the entrances into Scapa Flow. They used thick wire netting spread across certain areas to prevent U-boat penetration.

Admiral Karl Doenitz, the commander of all German U-boat fleets, requested a volunteer who would be willing to try to penetrate the Royal Navy's base and attack and sink as many ships as possible. Kapitan Gunter Prien was to become that volunteer, he would brave the heavily-guarded channels and the shallow waters to initiate this operation. On the night of 13th October 1939, *U-47* quietly crept into Scapa Flow, waiting in low tides then carefully avoiding antisubmarine nets. Eventually *U-47* got into position passing Lambs Holms, a small island. Prien raised his periscope, and to his disappointment there were only two ships in his sights. Scapa Flow was empty, except for *HMS Pegasus* and *HMS Royal Oak*, a training ship with a complement of 1,234 crew, mostly young boys who had only recently joined the Navy. They had not long retired to their bunks and hammocks, most of them were sleeping. At 0058 on 14th October, a large explosion was heard. Many were knocked out of their bunks and onto the floor. In the confusion, it was believed that the loud blast was something to do with the galley, and as they heard no more they went back to their beds. What in fact had happened was that *U-47* had fired a torpedo which probably hit an anchor chain. Prein's torpedo had missed its target. He decided to go around and try again at 0113 on 14th October. Three more torpedoes this time, and they struck home. The *HMS Royal Oak* rolled over and sank taking 833 men and boys with her. Headlines in the paper the next day shocked everyone. Who would have believed it would be possible to penetrate Scapa Flow? Then Gunter Prein, who safely made it back to his base in Germany was then awarded the Iron Cross.

Being an island nation, Britain cannot be self-sufficient. Unlike Germany, we rely on our trading routes to feed our people. These routes have been established over many hundreds of years, to the Americas, the Indies, Africa and beyond. The routes are Britain's arteries our merchant fleets are our lifeblood. Germany knew that this could be our Achilles heel: cut our arteries and starve Britain into submission. They first attempted this in the First World War and almost achieved their goal, this time they intended to finish the job. Their weapon was the U-boat. Prior to 1940, the only way that the Germans could get into the Atlantic Ocean to attack our merchant fleets and cut our supply lines, was to either risk the English Channel, which we made virtually impossible through our implementation of mine fields, or sail the North Sea across the top of Scotland, via the Faroe Isles south of Iceland. Owing to the length of the journey, they would need refuelling ships en route known as *Milchkühe* ("milk cows"). Stopping at these took time and could be dangerous in the north Atlantic. Milchkühe would hold all the stocks that a U-boat might require, including fuel, food, torpedoes, drinking water, and spare personnel to replace injured men.

With the fall of France in May 1940, Germany gained access to many Western ports in the Bordeaux region, which provided good access to the Atlantic Ocean. U-boat pens, massive garages for U-boats, were built. They were made of very thick concrete that could repel medium-sized bombs. This is where the U-boats could be serviced, refueled, restocked safely and made ready for their next sortie. The U-boat bases were at Brest, St Nazair, Lorient and La Rochelle and La Pallice. At Kernevel near to Brest was where Admiral Doenitz took over a French villa as a command base for all U-Boat operations. Kernevel was known as the "Sardine Can" because of its compact size and the amount of personnel who had to work there. It was here that the most deadly plans were put together, to attack and sink our merchant shipping to cut off the lifeblood of food and materials, and so to starve Britain out.

The main weapon was the type XIIC U-Boat. This relatively small craft at 800 tons, armed with fourteen torpedoes, two deck guns and with a crew of forty-four, would do untold damage to our merchant fleets. U-Boats or *"Unterseeboots"* were technically not submarines in the true sense. They were surface boats that were able to dive, prior to an attack then to hide submerged. They could also make an underwater getaway without being detected. The Type XIIC had a surface range of 6,500 miles, but only eighty miles when submerged. The plan was to have a group, or "pack" of twenty U-Boats, spread them out over a hundred miles, and scan the North Atlantic searching out our convoys of merchant shipping. These groups known as "wolf packs" would be in radio range of each other, although radio silence would be maintained to prevent them being located by the British direction-finding equipment installed on Royal Naval ships, and at land-based stations. As soon as a U-Boat in the pack spotted a target or convoy, a message would be sent to the others in the pack using a shortened code and navigational position from their short-signal code-book. The operator would then encrypt the message using their Enigma machine to disguise its content. Then this message would be sent by radio (Morse code), for the other U-boats in the pack to receive and decrypt. The other members of the pack would then vector into position until the target was in range, and then attack!

The Atlantic Gap

There was an area of sea approximately half-way across the North Atlantic that could not be reached by coastal command aircraft. It was well beyond their range. In those early days of the war, this area of sea was known as the Atlantic Gap, and was a safe haven for U-boats. For our merchant shipping to enter here, would have been to dice with death. The U-boats were able to sink them like shooting plastic ducks at the funfair. The Germans called this period Happy time", *Glückliche Zeit.* But merchant ships had little choice as this was the entry point to the western approaches into Britain. This deadly issue was not solved until early 1943, when the long-range "Liberator" aircraft, the biggest threat to U-boats, came on the scene. Later aircrafts were fitted with ASV (air-to-surface) Radar that could scan up to thirty miles ahead of the aircraft for enemy submarines.

At our wireless intercept stations, known as Y- stations, the U-boats' radio signals would be picked up. These very weak signals in standard international morse code were noted down by highly-skilled operators who were normally ladies of the armed services "WAFS", Wrens, and ATS. The signals were in code and could not be read. We recognised because of the radio frequencies used, that the signals were from U-boats. However, they were in code, and needed decryption, so they were packaged up then sent either by dispatch rider or teleprinter or both to Bletchley Park. Initially they were sent to the registry department for identification and logging, and then passed on to the team in Hut 8, the naval code-breaking Hut for deciphering. The Head of Hut 8 was the brilliant Cambridge mathematician Alan Turing, and his deputy was the British chess champion, also a brilliant mathematician, Hugh Alexander.

Together with other extremely clever personnel they formed a team of ace code-breakers. The Hut 8 department was responsible for extracting the plain German text from the intercepted gobbledygook. Once the text was identified as plain German, it was sent hastily to Hut 4 for translation and analysis. Once analysed, the German messages now known as ultra, would be sent by teleprinter down to the Operational Intelligence Centre at the Admiralty in London. The OIC is located deep down underneath Horse Guards' Parade. It was from here that Ned Denning & Roger Winn with the admiralty staff would track the U-Boats.

With the message translated, a plan was put into operation; a signal would be sent to the Commander of the appropriate fleet or convoy escort. The Commander would know that this was extremely reliable information. No mention of code-breaking would be uttered or thought of, but those in receipt of Ultra probably worked out the Intelligence behind the received signals. A letter was sent to "C", the head of MI6, to instruct that Churchill was to receive all naval decrypts ("naval ultra") from the code-breakers every day, delivered to him in a locked box. It is doubtful that this was actually done, since the Admiralty would probably not have wanted Churchill interfering with operations.

Owing to the extreme complexity of Naval Enigma, the code-breakers required more help with the system. When Frank Birch, head of Naval Section at Bletchley Park, gave the job of Head of Hut 8 naval code-breaking to Alan Turing, Birch said to Turing "You do realise that it has been said that it is impossible to break naval Enigma." Turing replied, "I like impossible tasks." It was clear that he would grab the chance to be in charge of his own department, and solve problems the way he wanted to attack them. He was probably also pleased to get away from his old boss Dilly Knox, who was driving Turing crackers with the constant noise in the cottage where he had been working.

Turing needed help and clues into this, the most difficult and complex Enigma system. He required a shopping list of items, short signal code-books, navigational positions codes, setting sheets (code-books, issued monthly) and any rotor wheels from the naval Enigma. At this time the German Naval Enigma operated with three rotors, and each rotor had a different wiring configuration. The German operator would have a set eight rotors from which he would choose three as per his daily setting instructions. Five of the eight rotors were the same as the standard German air force and army Enigma, which Bletchley Park had already obtained from some captured machines. So we were aware of their wiring, but at this stage we didn't have all eight rotors. That missing part of the job had to be completed with mathematical algorithms devised by Hut 8. This operation was extremely time-consuming using their current methods, but for Ultra to be of any real use, the team needed to be working faster.

A request was taken by Frank Birch to Harry Hinsley, the Chief liaison officer between Bletchley Park and the Admiralty. A plan was devised. We knew that the Germans had weather ships in the North Sea, and in the Atlantic, sending weather information back to the *Luftwaffe*, the *Kriegsmarine*, and also to the U-boat fleets. These weather ships were disguised as Norwegian fishing boats and were only very lightly armed. Early every morning they would send out the weather forecasts to the different services. Therefore it was known that these ships had Enigma on board with all the code-books to signal the different German military services. So attacks were planned, known as The Pinch, since it had to be quick and vicious. If the crew of the weather ship knew that it was being attacked, they would immediately dump their code-books into the sea, where they would perish as the ink was intentionally water soluble. The Enigma rotors would also be dumped into the sea and would sink straight to the bottom.

But we did attack, and we did retrieve many items required by the code-breakers. At Room 39, at the Admiralty in London, a naval commander planned a "pinch" called Operation Ruthless. The plan was to attack a German rescue boat and recover the secret documents onboard. It is not known where it came from, but the British were in possession of a *Heinkel* He111 bomber aircraft. The intention was to utilise our 30AU commando division, dress them in German uniforms, wrap mock blood-covered bandages around them, and fly the aircraft to a position where it could be rescued, then crash the aircraft into the sea in a controlled crash. This, incidentally, could not be done with this aircraft, since the Heinkel bomber has a glass and plastic front, which would smash and flood the aircraft as soon as it hit the water. Now, once the aircraft was in the water, the commander would call mayday in German. The Germans were very efficient in locating and recovering their air-crews brought down in the sea. The plan was to wait for the rescue vessel, and then jump aboard it, kill the crew, and sail the recue ship safely back to Britain along with the secret documents. "Operation Ruthless" was actually planned to go ahead, but due to bad weather conditions it was postponed, and eventually cancelled.

The plans were filed away under naval security, which had a prefix of "00-". It is possible it could have been filed under "007", which would have been very appropriate for this James Bond-style of operation. Even more appropriate, the man who dreamed it all up was a certain Commander Ian Fleming, the creator of James Bond. Fleming worked for the Director of naval intelligence, Admiral Godfrey and on some occasions, Fleming actually visited Hut 4 at Bletchley Park

Operation Primrose

9th May 1941, 300 miles south-west of Iceland, convoy OB318 comprising thirty-five merchant ships was travelling from Britain to the USA. Three of the Royal Navy escort ships *HMS Bulldog, HMS* Broadway both destroyers and *HMS Aubretia,* a corvette, were involved in this incident (the name 'Operation Primrose' was allocated after the incident had occurred). Joe Baker-Cresswell, the Captain of *HMS Bulldog* had received ultra from the Admiralty warning of U-boat activity in the area, which was rare this far west of Iceland. The convoy was being followed by *U-201* and *U-110*. The Commander of *U-110* was Kapitan Fritz Julius Lemp, the very same captain that sunk the passenger ship *SS Athenia* on the first day of the war. Lemp was held in high regard at U-boat headquarters, and known as one of the U-Boat ace commanders; in fact he could do no wrong, being Doenitz's 'blue-eyed boy'. However, he was about to get his comeuppance. He fired three torpedoes at the merchant ship Esmund and sank it. The crew of the Aubretia was immediately able to calculate the U-boat's location from the direction of the impact. They then spotted Lemp's periscope and chased the *U-110*, firing depth charges. *HMS Bulldog and HMS Broadway*, both destroyers, rushed to the scene. Lemp already had a technical balancing issue with *U-110*, and now to add to his problems he was being battered with depth charges from the escort's destroyers.

Realising that his U-boat was severely damaged and sinking, Lemp also believed that he was about to be rammed by *HMS Broadway* as he had seen her approaching at high speed towards him. He gave the order to 'abandon ship, and one of the radio operators, Georg Hugel, opted to go back and destroy the secret code-books and Enigma machine's rotors. Lemp told him to not worry about it as the boat was sinking and the secret equipment and code-books would go to the bottom. However, Hugel did go back on board, but only to retrieve a book of poems belonging to his girlfriend. Some of the crew dived into the sea but those remaining had access to the deck guns and could open fire. As the crew realised that *U-110* was not sinking and the ramming was not going to happen, the crew started to swim back to their U-Boat. This gave serious concern to Joe Baker-Cresswell, the Captain of *HMS Bulldog*, who had given the order to 'open fire'. Many of those remaining on the U-boat deck were shot. However, as they dived into the sea and swam to be rescued 'Cease fire' was ordered of his crew. Kapitan Lemp was never seen again, fifteen were killed or drowned in the sea, and there were thirty-two survivors taken prisoner.

U-110 did not sink as Lemp had predicted. Once the prisoners were on board and out of sight, sub Officer David Balme and eight of the crew from *HMS Bulldog* rowed a whaler boat (*long rowing boat*) across to *U-110* and boarded it. Once inside, they were concerned that the German crew may have left scuttling charges, but this seemed to not be the case. The emergency lights were glimmering blue, which lead Sub Lt Balme to the radio room where they found all of the signal and code-books along with an Enigma machine all intact. These were removed and pulled up through the conning tower to be brought aboard *HMS Bulldog*. Though *HMS Bulldog did* the important retrieval of the secret hoard, Captain Joe Baker-Cresswell informed *HMS Aubretia* that this was their official find and recorded in the logs as that. They decided to attempt to tow *U-110* back to Iceland, but unfortunately during the night it became low in the bow, the tow rope had to be cut and it was left to sink.

As *HMS Bulldog* sailed into Hvalfjord, Iceland, two Intelligence Officers from London were waiting for it. The code-books were photographed and Captain Baker-Cresswell and his men were told quite clearly, 'You saw nothing, you heard nothing. This is so secret and so important that we have wanted one of these since the start of the war.' (German military Enigma machine M3) On the 13th May 1941, the complete hoard from *U-110* went through the gates of Bletchley Park, into Hut 4 and was placed on the desk of Harry Hinsley, Chief liaison officer between Bletchley Park and the Admiralty. The vast majority of Britain's supplies: food, oil, grain and fuel were being transported across the North Atlantic Ocean by fleets of merchant shipping. Germany's plan was to sever our commercial trading routes and therefore starve Britain into submission.

Britain could not guard the complete north Atlantic with aircraft, as in the early years of the war aircraft range was limited. Our main ports were London, Liverpool, Southampton and Glasgow. To protect the Western approaches, a command centre was set up at Derby Street, Liverpool, by Admiral Martin Dunbar-Nasmith, who had been Commander-in-Chief, Plymouth. As Liverpool was susceptible to bombing, the command centre was built several story's underground. Admiral Percy Noble took over and was followed by Admiral Max Horton. It is here that they would also train captains how to escort shipping convoys. It was decided that the safest way for our merchant ships to cross the Atlantic was to sail in large groups known as convoys. The theory was that Royal Navy escort ships would surround the convoy, slow it down for stragglers but keep the convoy intact, whilst searching for lurking U-boats.

Ideally, the convoy could be kept moving at 10 to 12 knots, which with luck would keep it relatively safe, since a submerged U-boat had a maximum speed of only 7 knots. Accordingly, the Western Approaches Command Centre would plan convoys, give them identification numbers and navigation routing and assign escort ships. They would be linked with the Operational Intelligence Centre in London and would receive top secret ultra from Bletchley Park. In May 1941, reports were received from intelligence sources in Sweden and Norway of a German fleet breaking out of the Baltic into the North Sea and also of an unusually high number of radio signals coming from the same area. These signals recorded as Radio Traffic Analysis at Bletchley Park, were sent to the Operational Intelligence Centre at the Admiralty in London. It was confirmed shortly after, that the new German battleship Bismarck, along with the heavy cruiser *Prinz Eugen*, escorted by destroyers and *Luftwaffe* were heading towards the North Sea. This was the beginning of the German 'Operation Rhine', the full story of which will follow in a later chapter.

On 27th August 1941 Kapitan Hans Rahmlow, one of a new breed of young, inexperienced U-boat captains, was commanding *U-570*, eighty miles south of Iceland. Due to technical problems, the U-boat was unable to dive satisfactorily and after several attempts, *U-570* had to surface. Just at that moment, at 1300 hrs, flying overhead was a Hudson reconnaissance aircraft, and *HMS Burwell,* along with other vessels were close by. Kapitan Rahmlow realised the seriousness of the situation and informed U-boat Control, at

Kernevel. Then immediately as per his standard orders he destroyed the secret code-books and dumped the Enigma rotors into the sea. Had they succeeded in scuttling their U-boat early in this incident, they would all have all been picked up and taken as prisoners of war. But due to a delay, the British crew of *HMS Burwell* opened fire on the U-boat crew as a warning not to attempt to scuttle the ship as this would have been effectively committing suicide. The British took them as prisoners of war and towed *U-570* back to Iceland.

As the story appeared in the British Press, Doenitz was extremely concerned as to whether the British had found any coded documents on board. He contacted Erhard Maertens, head of the German Navy Communication Service, to ask whether the British would have been able to compromise the U-boat codes (Triton), if they had found any secret documents. Maertens came to the conclusion that the codes were safe, since the British did not know the special Keyword (*Stichwort*), which the German commanders were given verbally. This word, when applied to the Enigma settings would change the complete configuration of the machine, and this reassurance temporarily put Doenitz' mind at rest. What Maertens could not have known is that *Stichwort* made no difference to the code-breakers at Bletchley Park.

As far as *U-570* was concerned, the British renamed it *HMS Graph* and put it into active service with its new British crew. Unfortunately, an incident occurred that proved that we were not always masters of the sea. We almost lost a submarine *HMS Clyde,* but perhaps even more crucially, this episode initiated the Bletchley Park Blackout of the U-boat codes in the following February. "Ultra" signals were received at the Admiralty Operational Intelligence Centre (OIC) from Bletchley Park, giving details of a rendezvous of U-boats at Tarrafal Bay, off the Cape Verde Islands west of Senegal in late September 1941. *HMS Clyde* was at this time stalking a German tanker off the Canary Islands. Captain David Ingram was sent a signal to abort his operation and proceed to Terrafal Bay, where he should locate *U111, U68* and *U67*. They would be exchanging crew, stores, and torpedoes. This was an error, since the rules regarding the use of ultra clearly stated that the enemy must be made to think that any information gathered this way (and then acted upon) must have come from another source. Roger Winn at the OIC would have known this. There was always a danger that to act on any ultra signals could give away to the enemy that their signals were being read. When *HMS Clyde* arrived at the location, it was dark and they used their hydrophone to locate the enemy. Eventually *HMS Clyde* initiated an attack on the German U-boats. The attack was not successful, and *U67* crashed into *HMS Clyde's* stern, causing a water leak. This luckily was sealed, but then they had to return to Gibraltar for repairs.

A lucky escape, you may say. However, this incident was reported back to Admiral Doenitz, who immediately instituted an investigation as to how the British knew that the U-boats were to rendezvous at that exact time, and at that remote location. It was normally assumed that any breach in security was due to the action of spies. Doenitz once again called in the head of naval communications to investigate, but while Erhard Maertens insisted that the U-boat codes were impossible to break by the British, Doenitz was not convinced.In January 1942, Karl Doenitz had more important things to think about. Germany and Japan were allies and Germany was now at war with the United States. Operation *Paukenschlag*", Operation Drumbeat, was to follow.

Bletchley Park had given an indication that U-boats were in the vicinity at the US Eastern Seaboard. However, it appears that necessary precautions were not taken.

U-123, a type-IX long-range U-boat, was commanded by Kapitan Leutnant Reinhard Hardegen. He left his base at Lorient in France, with sealed orders on 18th December 1941, equipped with two New York tourist guides with fold-out maps of the harbour. As the fleet of U-boats exited the Bay of Biscay, routine signals were sent and intercepted by Y-stations. The signals were sent to Roger Winn at the Operational Intelligence Centre (OIC), via Bletchley Park. The U-boats were tracked as they were heading across the Atlantic, and Admiral Ernest King in the US was informed about this activity. However, it appears that little was done with the information provided. The Germans called this period, "The Second Happy time". *Glückliche zweiten Mal*

On 12th January, US Admiral Andrews was warned of an imminent attack by U-boats. This was a disaster for the US, as Kapitan Hardegen pulled into New York harbour to find all the harbour lights on. With a backdrop of lights from the New York skyline, he was able to locate the ships by their moving silhouettes. Hardegen's U 123 sank seven ships, totalling 46,744 tons, before running out of torpedoes. A total of twenty-three ships were sunk, costing many thousands of tons of freight, and many lost lives. The attacks continued with more convoys of U-boats targeting areas from Canada, and as far south as the Caribbean. The Germans lost many U-boats, but the US was caught napping.

The Penny Drops

The 1941 successes of U-Boat destruction by the allies caused Admiral Doenitz to consider the possibility that the German U-Boat codes had possibly been compromised. The head of German Naval Communications assured Doenitz that it was highly improbable that the allies would be able to read naval Enigma, even if they obtained some documents. Nevertheless, Doenitz refused to believe that espionage was to blame, as was the common theory of the time. Doenitz ordered a more secure system, which led to the addition of a fourth rotor to the standard 3-rotor naval Enigma machine, with a new short-signal code-book. This was introduced into service on 1st February 1942. From that date, Bletchley Park were no longer able to read the U-boat codes. The code-breakers called this period "The BP Blackout". We were losing the Battle of the Atlantic before this episode, and now we were in real trouble, and things were going to get worse.

The effects of the "BP Blackout"

The staff at Bletchley Park knew that they were in a war. They also appreciated that, apart from one small incident in November 1940, they were not being bombed. They were not subjected to rationing, and whilst they were aware that their relatives and friends in the cities were having a terrible time in the Blitz, life was relatively good in Bletchley Park. A peaceful life of green spaces, and plenty of food. They were not all aware of the exact work they were dealing with, but they all had a jolly good idea. Secrecy was the essence, as well as having good times. They also knew that the work they were involved with was saving lives. They enjoyed a nice friendly atmosphere and the good life.

This was until 1st February 1942, when everything changed. We were no longer able to track the U-boats owing to the change in security procedures to the naval U-boat system. Britain being an island race could only survive if we were able to be fed by our trading routes to the world. Hitler knew this was our weak point and by severing our arteries of supply ships with the deadly U-boats, ensured that we were losing the war. Of course, you have to be able to replace more ships and crews than you are losing, but this was not happening and we were losing thousands of tons of shipping every week. Now we were unable to even locate where the U-boat "Wolf-packs" (*collective term for U-Boats attacking a convoy*) were congregating and waiting to pounce. The atmosphere at Bletchley Park changed overnight, doom and gloom set in. The pressure was now on, especially in Hut 8, which up until now had been relatively successful at breaking the U-boat codes. Staff were reading the newspapers and realising how important their jobs were.

The chiefs at the Admiralty visited Bletchley Park wanting to know when the U-boat code would be able to be read again. The British called this code "Shark", whilst the official German name was "Triton". There was never an easy relationship with the Admiralty, since the code-breaking facility (NID25) at Room 40 was snatched away from them by Lord Curzon in 1919. Eventually it was put into the hands of a civilian organisation at the offices of the Secret Intelligence Service (MI6). Now at Bletchley Park known as the Government Code & Cipher School, the pressure was now on. The heads of the GC&CS told the Admirals that there was no easy solution and no possible idea when we could be back into Shark. As the disappointed Admirals left, one of them made the comment "This is a great day for Adolf Hitler" and then returned to London.

Piece of luck

We needed a miracle, and needed it quick. With a stroke of luck, it came. Just as it was calculated that, Britain had only six weeks-worth of supplies of food left, before more draconian rationing would have to take place.

30th October 1942 in the Eastern Mediterranean, between Haifa and 70 miles north of Port Said, a Sunderland aircraft, equipped with air-to-surface vessel radar (ASV), picked up the trail of a lurking U-Boat. *HMS Hero,* a destroyer picked up the Sunderland's radio broadcast and marked the spot until *HMS Petard* and *HMS Dulverton* arrived on the scene, along with *HMS Pakenham.* The Destroyers chased the U-boat for 10 hours, using ASDIC, a type of Sonar, as well as by spotting the tell-tale periscope. Eventually the U-boat was depth-charged. It was sitting 150 feet below the surface, well below its safety level, being pounded by the explosions, eventually brought to the surface at 2240, possibly through lack of air.

It turned out to be U559. Captain Thornton of *HMS Petard* ordered his crew to man the machine guns. U559 was illuminated by searchlights from *HMS Petard*. If anyone from the U-boat crew were to emerge from their boat, and be seen about to dump any documents or machines into the sea, they were to immediately open fire at the conning tower hatch. Before the crew abandoned *U-559*, they tried to open the sea cocks to flood the boat, which would have sent it to the bottom quite quickly, but the mechanism was jammed because of the depth-charge damage, and failed to operate effectively. The U-boat crew were being taken prisoners by the way of a whaler boat and were then blind-folded and taken below. Then, First Lieutenant Anthony Fasson, Able Seaman Colin Grazier, and Tommy Brown, a 16-year old NAAFI assistant who lied about his age to join the Navy, dived into the sea and swam across to board the fated U-boat.

As some of the German prisoners were being taken onto *HMS Petard*, they saw the British seamen board *U-559*. This is when they realised that they should have destroyed the secret documents. Inside *U-559*, the water was - pouring in through damage holes in the conning tower, as the British seamen made their way down it. The U-boat's control room was waist-deep in a mixture of seawater, sewage and rotten floating food. There was a terrible stench of chlorine gas amongst other smells. This was a reaction of the seawater and battery acid. There was no emergency blue lighting so they had to use their flashlight torches. They made their way to the radio room to find the drawers and cupboards locked. Fasson used a machine gun to shoot off the locks, and as they searched the drawers and shelves, they discovered secret documents. These were carefully kept dry as Tommy Brown took them up the ladder with sea water pouring down on him and handed them to Ken Lacroix an ASDIC operator, who was waiting at the top of the conning tower. Lacroix passed the retrieved documents down carefully to a waiting whaler boat that had now come along side. Shortly afterwards a further two packages of documents were brought up by Brown.

As the U-boat was starting to list, Fasson and Grazier were attempting to remove a machine which resembled a typewriter in a casing which was bolted down. Tommy Brown and Lacroix warned them to abandon what they were doing immediately and come out. They were continuing to attempt the removal. Brown who again was inside the boat went back up the ladder to see the position of the U-boat, he then again shouted down to Fasson and Grazier to 'get out now!' The U-boat started to keel over, Tommy Brown and Ken Lacroix dived clear. Fasson and Grazier became trapped in the rungs of the ladder as *U-559* slipped beneath the waves and sank, taking the two extremely brave seamen with her. Brown and Lacroix were very lucky to not be dragged down with the U-boat. Anthony Fasson and Colin Grazier were both posthumously awarded the George Cross for this operation. Tommy Brown received the George Medal, and Ken Lacroix was mentioned in despatches. Winston Churchill was informed of the retrieved hoard of code-books and later said that this small operation changed the course of the war.

Beginning of the end

The code-books were back at Bletchley Park on 24th November 1942. By 13th December 1942, staff at Hut 8 were once again able to read the U-boat Enigma. U-boat locations and information was sent by Bletchley Park to the Operations Intelligence Centre in London. Now with the added assistance of the long range aircraft, "the Liberator", the Atlantic gap was covered, and many U-boats were being successfully hunted down. The day of the U-boats' dominance in the Atlantic was coming to an end. By May 1943, Doenitz had lost over one hundred U-boats in just a few months. He had also lost his son who was a member of the crew on one of the boats. By the end of May, Admiral Doenitz recalled all U-boats from the North Atlantic. He claimed that it was only a suspension until the new high technology U-boats ("Type XXI") became available. Fortunately, they were not ready until the final days of the war.

The remaining Atlantic U-boats were re-deployed to Norway and the Mediterranean. This enabled the British and Americans to bring personnel, armaments and fuel from the US to start the build-up for the Allied invasion of Europe, Operation Overlord (D-day). Also, they were then able to bring in urgently needed provisions to ease the severe rationing currently being endured by the British people. Hostile operations continued in the Atlantic until the end of the war, although the major threat had, for the time being, been averted. Just before the end of the war, the Germans had made many technical advances, such as the V1 and V2 rockets and the jet fighter aircraft.

There was also a new high-tech Type XXI U-Boat. There was not a great difference between the U-boats of WW1 and WW2, both of these had to spend the majority of their time sailing on the surface. To dive, U-boats had to switch from their diesel-powered engines, which required air, to electric propulsion which relied on batteries. This limited their range because they needed to return to the surface so those batteries could be recharged. However, in some of the later Types VII-C and IX-C, a snorkel was retro-fitted. The snorkel would then be raised above the surface providing an air intake to allow the U-boat to utilise its diesel engines while still submerged and to replenish the breathable air for the crew.

The Type XXI U-boat was different. They incorporated a completely new concept in submarines. They were fuelled by hydrogen peroxide (H_2O_2), which is commonly known as a small, harmless bottle of hair bleach that can be purchased from your local pharmacy. However, in its concentrated form, H_2O_2 when compressed becomes an extremely volatile propellant. This was an experimental design to utilise the revolutionary new propulsion system developed by Dr Helmuth Walter. Hydrogen peroxide was broken down using a catalyst to provide steam and oxygen, which were then mixed with water and diesel fuel, and the mixture combusted. The resultant products were very high temperature steam and pressurised carbon dioxide, which drove a turbine. This experimental U-boat could achieve 26 knots whilst submerged, compared with 7-8 knots of a conventional U-boat. Four U-boats of this type were produced. All were used solely as test boats of superior quality, but all four had numerous teething problems, often associated with revolutionary new designs, and were eventually laid up and finally scuttled in 1945.

After World War II several navies attempted to continue development of the Walter turbine. In the end, they all dropped the design as too dangerous. Most did, however, adopt many of Professor Walter's ideas when it came to hull design. The development of nuclear reactors small enough to use in a submarine in the 1950s permanently terminated Hydrogen Peroxide propulsion research except for torpedoes. Most countries have now given up on those as well. A defective hydrogen peroxide fuelled torpedo is suspected as the primary cause of the sinking of the Russian submarine Kursk in 2000. This new U-boat was introduced too late to be of any real use during WW2 but many were still in production. After the war, the uncompleted Type XXIs were scrapped but the completed ones were shared amongst the allies and were operational into the 1950s.

The Rubber Sub

October 1943 saw yet another breakthrough, stealth technology, which was achieved by using a coating of synthetic rubber tiles incorporating small holes (code-named Alberich after a German mythological dwarf that could make itself invisible). The *U-480*, the stealth U-boat Type VII-C was virtually invisible to ASDIC Sonar. The Germans developed a 4-millimetre (0.16 in) thick sheet of synthetic rubber that attenuated sound in the 10 to 18 kHz range to 15% of its normal strength. This frequency range matched the operating range of the early ASDIC active sonar used by the Allies. ASDIC's operating range would have been correspondingly reduced from its optimal range of 2,000 metres (6,600ft) to somewhere around 300 meters (980ft). The rubber contained a series of holes, which helped break up sound waves. There were problems with this technology: the material performed differently at different depths, due to the holes being compressed by water pressure, and securing the tiles to the submarine's hull required a special adhesive and careful application. The first tests were conducted in 1940, but it was not used operationally until 1944, with *U-480*. According to the Naked Science television episode "Stealth Submarine", *U-480* had a perforated inner rubber layer covered by a smooth outer one. This formed air pockets with the right separation and size to muffle sonar waves. This experimental boat was being tested in the English Channel when it disappeared. Sunk between January 29th and February 20th 1945 in minefield Brazier D2 in the English Channel, with the loss of the entire crew of 48. *U-480* was subsequently discovered near the Isle of Wight by divers in 1997, having fallen victim to a mine which damaged its tail, sending it to the bottom.

By 1943 Adolf Hitler was extremely disappointed with his surface fleet of ships which were continually being bombed, torpedoed and sunk. Their success, compared with that of the U-boats was minimal, however due to the costs of harbouring, funding and materials, the surface fleet was becoming a burden. Subsequently, on 30th January 1943, ten years to the day after he took power, Hitler dismissed Grand Admiral Erich Raeder, the Head of the *Kriegsmarine*, and promoted Admiral Karl Doenitz to the position of Grand Admiral. Doenitz was later to become Hitler's deputy after Hitler's suicide. Interestingly it was General Alfred Jodl not Doenitz who signed the peace treaty with the Allies on 7th May 1945. 30th January 1943 was a great day for Bletchley Park because Hitler had ordered that the message of Doenitz' promotion should be sent to every military unit across the *Wehrmacht*, thus ensuring mass duplication of the message. This was known by our code-breakers as an "in-depth crib" (clue), meaning that if the message could be read on one network, the same message could be read on another network. Due to Hitler's incredible blunder, all messages on most networks could be read that day.

The 1981 Columbia film *"Das Boot"* offers an extremely good insight into the life on board a U-boat. Directed by Wolfgang Petersen, the film describes the claustrophobic world of a WWII German U-boat: the boredom, the filth, and the sheer terror. Only a few U Boats survive today, as you can well imagine. If you would like to see one, the best preserved is *U-505* in the Museum of Science and Industry Chicago, USA. You could also visit *U-995* in Laboe Naval Memorial northern Germany. Closer to home is the *U-534* at the U Boat Story Museum at Birkenhead, Merseyside, England.

HMS GLORIOUS incident

HMS Glorious was originally built in 1915 as a battle cruiser at Harland & Wolff, Belfast. In 1924 it was decided to convert her to an aircraft carrier. This was due to the 1922 Washington Naval Treaty as it was calculated that Britain had excess tonnage in capital war ships. The Washington Treaty was an arms limitation agreement for warships, later amended by the 1935 London Naval Treaty. This all significantly reduced British naval power. Japan and Italy pulled out of the agreement after the 1935 London Treaty.

HMS Glorious was 22,360 tons, with a speed of thirty-one knots, and as an aircraft carrier had a complement of 1,245 crew. On this particular operation there were thirty-six aircraft onboard: six Swordfish torpedo planes, ten Hurricanes, ten Sea Gladiators, and ten RAF Gladiators. In June 1940, she was assisting the evacuation of troops from Norway, known as operation Alphabet. This particular voyage was to have been her fifth in this operation. In the early hours of 8th June 1940, while sailing to Scapa Flow along with *HMS Ark Royal* and escort destroyers *HMS ardent* and *HMS Acasta,* Captain D'Oyly-Hughes of *HMS Glorious* requested to speed up and leave Ark Royal. He was due to attend a Court Martial in which he was giving evidence to an incident which occurred on a previous trip. This was to be held at Scapa Flow. *HMS Glorious* along with the destroyers sped away at seventeen knots zig-zagging in a anti-submarine path. None of the three ships were equipped with Radar or had lookouts in the crows nest. Meanwhile, at Bletchley Park, Harry Hinsley was in charge of liaison at Hut 4 with the Operational Intelligence Centre (OIC) at the Admiralty in London. Hinsley was receiving reports of 'Traffic Analysis' which were showing high volumes of radio traffic coming from the Baltic Area. This information was not from deciphered radio messages, but from high frequency direction findings which produced enemy movement reports. The reports indicated that capital German ships were exiting the Baltic and breaking into the North Sea and heading north. Hinsley immediately informed the OIC. The Admiralty seemed not to be concerned that this was an impending danger to our ships. Harry Hinsley sent a second communication as it was becoming clear that our fleet would be in danger if evasive action was not taken. It was possible that since the Germans hadn't been too involved in that area yet, the British were becoming complacent, and were off their guard Once again, the OIC were not convinced that this young graduate could possibly understand the complexities of naval issues and the negative response from the Admiralty continued. With increasing frustration, Harry Hinsley continued to receive traffic analysis reports, knowing that they were being ignored. He implored the OIC to acknowledge the reports but, inexplicably, the Admiralty again declined to act.

As *HMS Glorious* was unaware of this activity, Captain D'Oyly-Hughes was enjoying the calm seas and good weather. During summer inside the Arctic Circle, there are twenty-four hours of daylight. A complacent *HMS Glorious* failed to deploy spotter planes, which was unusual for an aircraft carrier, and would have given an all-round view of approximately forty miles. Then at 16:00 hours, two unknown ships were spotted on the horizon. Action stations were called at 16:20. Unbeknown to Captain D'Oyly-Hughes, two German battle-cruisers, the *Scharnhorst* and her sister ship the *Gneisenau,* were heading directly towards his ship and accompanying destroyers *HMS Ardent* and *HMS Acasta.* The first attack was at 16:32, and sadly by 18:20 all three British ships were lost The Admiralty had ignored Harry Hinsley's warnings. Captain Guy D'Oyly-Hughes was previously a sub-mariner and had limited experience on aircraft carriers. There were thirty-six aircraft plus their pilots, a total of 1,548 men and officers were on the British ships, and there were only thirty-nine survivors. At 17.15 hrs GMT on 8th June 1940, the German warships *Scharnhorst* and *Gneisenau* spotted *HMS Glorious* at fifteen miles. Glorious sent an urgent radio message that the Germans intercepted, which the British at Narvik Communications Centre never received, however, it was too late. The German battle cruisers were to soon sink all the British ships. Nothing was known about the incident until a German radio news broadcast on the following morning, 9th June 1940. Ned Denning at the Admiralty telephoned Harry Hinsley at 2pm that day, admitting that his information had indeed been correct. Regrettably, even today, the Admiralty is insistent that at the time of the incident, there was not enough evidence to signal the fleet.

Admiral Marschall on *Scharnhorst* was relieved of his duty for disobeying orders. As their instruction was to specifically attack shipping at Harstad. The charge laid against him regarded wasting ammunition and putting his ships at risk. Both *Scharnhorst* and *Gneisenau* had damage after this affair.

On the return to Germany the submarine *HMS Clyde* caused series damage to *Gneisenau* and consequently they were out of action for months.

Channel Dash February 1942

After active service commerce-raiding in the North Atlantic, attacking British merchant fleets, three German warships were being repaired in Brest, France. Commerce-raids were mainly achieved by fleets of U-boats, which were very successful, and backed up with the capital warships *KM Prinz-Eugen* and *KM Scharnhorst,* along with her sister ship *KM Gneisenau.* These were now being repaired and made ready for more sorties in the Atlantic. Owing to continued British bombing raids, every time the ships were repaired, they were again damaged, so it was made impossible for them to get back to work in the Atlantic. Adolf Hitler had enough on his plate with his armies being bogged down on the Russian front and now his capital warships were becoming a burden. Especially now as the U-Boats were having a great success with Operation Drumbeat, the attack on the Eastern Seaboard of the United States. Also, there were fewer attacks on U-Boats due to the Germans changing the codes of the Enigma cipher system (new code called Triton), introducing a new "short signal code-book" and adding a forth rotor to the Enigma machine itself. Although introducing these measures, the Germans were never convinced that their Enigma codes had ever been compromised. Hitler demanded that all the warships at Brest were returned to Germany for repairs before they became completely unserviceable. Command of this operation was to be by Vice Admiral Otto Ciliax (Type Commander, Battleships) who would fly his flag on *Scharnhorst.* The main control would come under Group West in Paris by General Admiral Saalwachter.

The Plan

Though it was believed by the Germans that their signals were impossible to read they realised that an increase in radio traffic would alert the enemy. Therefore, for this operation, radio silence was to be maintained. The original route was to sail via the Denmark straits, but this long haul between Greenland and Iceland would take far too long. Because Hitler was impatient for this operation to be completed, he told his Admirals to use the English Channel. The Channel was probably the most protected and fortified strip of seaway anywhere in the world. The plan was to catch the British napping and sail past the narrowest part, Dover, at high speed in broad daylight. As a deception for any would-be French spies, just prior to the operation, the word was put out in bars and cafes that the German ships were planning to sail to the

Mediterranean. The local people were to see hot-weather clothing being bought in shops and delivered to the docks. This was all part of the cover.

02:15 on the 11th February 1942, Operation Cerberus, what we now call the "Channel Dash", was put into operation. The German ships, along with the cover of the *Luftwaffe* and patrolling U-boats, and the torpedo boats known as E-boats, made a dash along the English Channel. They were spotted by Spitfire pilots, who had been ordered to maintain radio silence, so they could not report what they had seen to anyone until they returned to their base later that day. The British were caught with their pants down, from faulty radar systems, to the absence of six destroyers which were in the North Sea on a training exercise. The German fleet sailed through the straits of Dover as bold as brass. Our shore-based gun batteries failed to score any hits. The saddest thing of all is that we sent up six Fairey Swordfish torpedo planes, which had played such a fantastic role in May 1941 to stop the Bismarck, to be completely obliterated in this suicidal attack on this such-powerful armada, backed up with the *Luftwaffe*. Even General Admiral Ciliax remarked on the bravery of the crew of those ancient-looking bi-planes. Admiral Ramsey, who was commanding the British part of this operation, suffered the destruction of forty-two of our aircraft. *HMS Worcester*, a destroyer, was also badly damaged, leaving twenty-four dead and forty-five wounded.

What should have easily been a success story was a complete disaster for the morale of the British coastal command and an embarrassment for the Royal Navy. As far as the German ships were concerned, General Admiral Ciliax got them all back to Germany in one piece, but only just. There were some incidents on the last stretch. *Scharnhorst* hit two mines, causing damage which took three months to repair and bring back into service. *Gneisenau* hit a mine, which knocked out an engine turbine for a short period, but it did make the journey back to Kiel. Later that year Hitler decided he wanted all his surface fleet scrapped due to their poor performance and extremely high costs. Grand Admiral Erich Raeder did not agree with Hitler and he was eventually replaced. In January 1943 the new Grand Admiral Karl Doenitz persuaded Hitler that it would be more costly to scrap them than to keep them.

Scharnhorst was sent to Norway as a deterrent of a possible invasion by the British (this was part of a British deception), and it was eventually sunk by *HMS Duke* of York, *HMS Belfast* and *HMS Jamaica* in December 1943. This thorn in the side of the Royal Navy, was at last put to rest. In 1979 Norway offered to return one of the gun turrets of *Scharnhorst* to Germany, which was in Trondheim at the time. The offer was rejected, the gun turret was instead preserved as a museum piece in Norway.

Prinz-Eugen departed *Swinemünde* for Copenhagen, arriving on 20th April, there she was decommissioned on 7th May and turned over to Royal Navy control. On 27th May 1945, *Prinz Eugen* and the light cruiser *Nürnberg*—the only major German naval vessels to survive the war—were escorted by the British cruisers Dido and Devonshire to Wilhelmshaven.

On 13th December, *Prinz Eugen* was awarded as a war prize to the United States, which sent the ship to *Wesermünde*. The United States did not particularly want the cruiser, but it did want to prevent the Soviet Union from acquiring it. The cruiser was commissioned into the US Navy as the unclassified miscellaneous vessel *USS Prinz Eugen*. The US navy used it in Operation Crossroads in the Central Pacific to test the effects of a nuclear bomb on battleships. On 22nd December, *Prinz Eugen* capsized and sank.

Gneisenau was finally put out of action for good after a heavy bombing raid at Kiel on 26–27th February 1942. She was badly damaged in the air raid, and *Gneisenau* remained unused in Gotenhafen until the end of the war. As the Red Army advanced on the city, the remaining crew took the ship out to the entrance of the harbor and sank the vessel as a blockship on 27 March 1945. In 1947, the Polish government ordered the ship be removed, and initial salvage operations began. The ship was sealed and refloated on 12th September 1951, and was then completely scrapped, although it is believed that some of her steel was used in the construction of Polish merchant vessels. She was the largest ship raised at the time.

Alan Turing the Man Who knew too much

Alan Turing was born on 23rd June 1912, at 2 Warrington Crescent, Maida Vale near Paddington in West London, now The Colonnade Hotel. His parents, being typical colonials, at times lived in India. His father was a civil servant in the Indian high commission, with a religious family background. His mother's family was of an engineering background. They were involved in the building and maintenance of the Madras Railway. Alan, along with his older brother John, was put out to foster in England with a retired army couple in St Leonards-on-sea in Sussex. At a very early age, Alan would experiment by planting toy soldiers in the garden to see if the broken arms and legs would grow back. Also, during a sports day at St Michael's Infants school, Alan paid no interest in the hockey that his friends were playing, choosing instead to stare at the daisies and wonder, watching them grow.

Someone once gave the young Alan a gift of a book called "Natural Wonders Every Child Should Know", and this opened his eyes to the world of science. Alan went on from St Michael's to Hazlehurst Prep School, which his father hoped would lead him into public school, like his brother John who was already at Marlborough.

Alan's father was very British and patriotic, but for tax reasons he preferred to live in France in between his trips to India. However, he insisted that his children go through the education of the English public school tradition, and he managed to get Alan a place at Sherbourne School in Dorset.

Education

On Alan's first day at this prestigious school, he was late. In fact, he was a day late. But he did have rather a good excuse, since it was on 4th May 1926, the first day of the national strike. The 14-year-old Alan had just arrived back to Southampton after a short holiday with his parents at their home in France. Finding no transport available, he decided to leave his luggage with an instruction to deliver it to Sherbourne School, whilst he got on his bike and cycled there. He split the sixty mile journey into two parts with an overnight stay in Blanford Forum, where an innkeeper took in this 14-year-old schoolboy. The following day, he finally arrived at Sherbourne.

Alan found it difficult to make friends and was often unhappy, which was often reflected in poor academic performance and results. He struggled with many of the subjects to the extent that his father was called in to discuss Alan's poor school report with the Headmaster. The Headmaster suggested to Alan's father that, if Alan was not interested in languages or the classics then maybe Sherbourne School was not for him. The following year, things started to pick up for Alan. He had met a new friend, Christopher Morcom, and the two boys got on extremely well together, with common interests in science, nature and mathematics. They would read and digest Einstein's theories and jot formulae down the sides of pages of their school textbooks, such as Shakespeare or Dickens.

Alan and Christopher went everywhere together and they both planned to eventually get into Trinity College, Cambridge. This being any mathematician's dream since it had been the college of Sir Isaac Newton. On their way to Cambridge to sit the entrance examination, December 1929, they visited Christopher's mother's art studio in London. Alan and Christopher shared a pear there, cut with a knife made of a toxic metal called vanadium. Alan later wrote about this incident with "deadly stuff" in a letter to his mother. A few weeks later, the results from Cambridge were received. Alan was devastated to find that he had failed the entrance exam, but that his best friend Christopher had passed and was accepted into Trinity. Sadly, things were still yet to deteriorate for the young Turing.

Early in 1930, Christopher Morcom went on holiday with his parents in Yorkshire. While they were there, Christopher became very ill and was admitted into hospital with a form of tuberculosis. His condition became critical, and on 13th February 1930 Christopher Morcom died. Alan was now absolutely devastated. No Cambridge and now no friend. Superficially, Alan seemed to cope with this situation, but it has been suggested that he in fact never recovered from this loss, and always remained close friends with Christopher's mother. Alan channelled his energies into hard and focussed studying and eventually won a scholarship to King's College, Cambridge in 1931.

At Cambridge, Alan also became interested in athletics. Rowing, cycling and running everywhere he could. He won races and was a real champion. Had it not been for his mathematics, he would almost certainly have competed in the Olympic Games. He continued this active lifestyle throughout his life, and if he was to attend a meeting many miles away, he would cycle there or even run.

Alan Turing turned to studying some very rare issues of pure mathematics. One of his main lecturers was M A H Newman (Max Newman), a name that was to feature heavily later on in Alan's life.Turing studied the works of David Hilbert and Kurt Gödel, 19th century mathematicians and logisticians looking at the *Entscheidungsproblem* or Decision Problem. This was to question and break down the logic of what we might consider simple and irrefutable theories and equations. A very crude example would be $2 + 2 = 4$. How do we know that? Is it accurate? If not, what is the true answer? He was also reading "Principia Mathematica" (Whitehead & Russell, 1910). Eventually, Turing invented a hypothetical machine that could solve any mathematical problem with the use of unlimited reels of paper. The Turing machine has become the foundation of the modern theory of computation and computability.

What followed was a groundbreaking paper on 6th November 1936 called "Computable numbers with an application to the *Entscheidungsproblem*", which was published by the London Mathematical Society. Initially it was rejected as there was already a paper covering similar theories, written by an American mathematician Alonzo Church, but after challenging the decision, it became clear that there were significant differences.

Princeton

Turing graduated with his first class honours degree in 1934. He was elected a Fellow of King's in March 1935, at the age of only twenty-two. As well as publishing his historic paper in 1936, he also won a Smith's Prize for work on probability theory, and he might then have seemed on course for a successful career as a mildly eccentric King's don engaged in pure mathematics. He decided to take his PhD at the Department of Advanced Mathematics at Princeton University, New Jersey, USA. He even studied under Alonzo Church as well as Hungarian born Jon von Neumann. While at Princeton, Turing invented a cipher machine and also improved his mechanical Hypothetical Calculating Computer, now renamed the "Universal Turing Machine". This machine now included the principle of changing components within it, so that different sets of mathematical problems could be calculated. This seems to have been an early version of the "stored programme" concept.

Turing obtained his PhD in 1938 and was offered a part-time job at Princeton University by Jon von Neumann. Turing declined the offer and instead returned to Cambridge University to continue his research fellowship at King's College.

In 1938 something else was happening, war with Germany was brewing. In March 1939 the Prime Minister Neville Chamberlain had signed the Polish military alliance which guaranteed Britain's support for Poland should Germany invade. Everyone felt that war was just around the corner.

In Germany, Adolf Hitler's master plan, known as "The Final Solution" aimed to eliminate all the Communists and Jews from Europe. Jewish people tried their best to flee from Germany to the United States, Britain or anywhere they could to get away from the Nazis. There were several charities set up to rescue children whose parents were themselves unable to escape. At King's College, Professor Clapman chaired a committee to receive Jewish refugees who were allowed in by the government. Turing was friends with Fred Clayton, a teacher at a school in Dresden. There were two particular Jewish boys at that school whose mother desperately wanted to send to the safety of England. With the assistance of the Quakers Relief Action, they were brought to a refugee camp at Harwich, where Turing cycled to meet Fred Clayton. One of the boys, Robert Augenfeld desperately wanted to become a chemist from a very early age, and Clayton was keen for Turing to assist with his teaching, which he certainly did. Knowing the right contacts helped Augenfield into Rossall public school in Lancashire. Rossall School decided to take a number of refugees without any fees. Fred sponsored the boy's brother Karl who also was accepted at Rossall School. The full episode of this can be found in Andrew Hodges' biography of Alan Turing, "Alan Turing the enigma".

The war years

Meanwhile in mid-1939, the Government Code and Cipher School (GC&CS), a part of the Secret Intelligence Service (MI6), was on the verge of moving out of London to a safe haven in North Buckinghamshire at Bletchley Park where they were working towards breaking into the German military radio communications which had been enciphered into an unreadable text using a machine called Enigma.

The Germans considered their military Enigma system impossible to break, so the GC&CS went on the offensive and searched the universities for what the Chief of MI6, Admiral Sinclair, called the "Professor type". These were to be the highest grade of brilliant mathematicians, linguists and intellectuals to attack this problem. High-ranking officials of the GC&CS, The Chief Alistair Denniston; Professor of History, Frank Adcock; and Head of Naval section, Frank Birch - visited Oxford and Cambridge universities. We believe it was probably veteran WW1 code-breaker Adcock who first located Alan Turing. Turing was then asked that should there be the possibility of a war with Germany, would he consider working for the government on a very secret project. Although Alan was a pacifist at heart he definitely wanted to help his country should a war ensue. He was invited to the offices of the GC&CS, based at 54 Broadway Buildings, Westminster London, and once he had signed the official secrets act, he was shown the problems he would be working on. Turing then returned to Cambridge.

When Hitler's troops marched into Poland on the 1st September 1939, Prime Minister Chamberlain gave Germany until 11am on the 3rd September to withdraw or "a state of war would exist between us". When the deadline passed, Britain was once again at war with Germany. At 8am on Monday 4th September 1939, Alan Turing walked through the gates of Bletchley Park, the wartime home of the GC&CS, for the first time. After an interview with Commander Alistair Denniston the Director of the GC&CS, Turing was put to work at the cottage in the Stable Yard. His new boss would be the extremely eccentric Alfred Dilwyn "Dilly" Knox, an Egyptologist by profession as well as a veteran code-breaker from WW1, when Room 40 at the Old Admiralty Buildings was the headquarters of naval code-breaking.

German military Enigma was posing a massive problem for even the hardened code-breakers. Whilst there were many different setting sheets for different sections of the German military *(wehrmacht)*, the German army and air force were using the same machine with similar setting procedures. Due to simple setting errors combined with short cuts taken by many lazy Enigma operators who continually bucked their own system, it was possible to break the German Enigma on a regular basis (*See Polish chapter*). Turing realised that the

Germans would soon plug this gap, and the British would lose this advantage. Sure enough, in May 1940 as the German armies marched into France, the systems were changed. The chances of breaking each daily key (starting position) was 159 million million million (159^{18}), then on top of this each individual message had its own setup procedure. Alan Turing said "this needle in a haystack could only be found by removing the hay".

Alan Turing went about inventing what he called the "Bombe machine", an unfortunate name for a machine in the time of war. It was loosely based on the name of a Polish machine "the Bomby". The invaluable Polish code-breakers gave the British a copy of the German military Enigma machine which they built themselves, from the details supplied by a German traitor.

Turing's Bombe machine worked but it had some problems. It was an electro-mechanical device which emulated up to thirty-six Enigma machines running at high speed. The design was amended by Gordon Welchman's "Diagonal Board". Welchman was another brilliant Cambridge mathematician, who eventually became the head of Hut 6.

The Bombe machine now was working effectively and throughout the war was an integral part of Enigma code-breaking. Many hundreds of them were required to cope with the amount of messages that were pouring into Bletchley Park from the wireless intercept stations known as Y stations). The Germans and other Axis countries were now operating on almost two hundred Enigma networks. Due to the extreme secrecy of this project, it was impossible to obtain funding for these Bombe machines through normal government channels. In order to short-cut the standard procedures, Alan Turing and Gordon Welchman, along with their deputies, composed a letter to be sent directly to Prime Minister Winston Churchill, who had recently visited Bletchley Park on the 6th September 1941. The letter, which was personally delivered to 10 Downing Street by one of the code-breakers, asked for funding for hundreds of these Bombe machines to be built by the British Tabulating Machine company at Letchworth Garden City in Hertfordshire. Funding would also be required for running costs, and for the Wrens and the RAF to operate and maintain the machines. Churchill saw how valid and urgent this project was, and processed their request as "ACTION THIS DAY", and the funds for building the Bombes were at last allowed.

Frank Birch, head of the naval section at Bletchley Park, interviewed Turing and offered him the position of head of the naval code-breaking section. When Turing agreed, Birch advised him that the German Naval Enigma had been dubbed "impossible" to break. Turing replied, "I like impossible tasks". What he probably meant was that it would be great to get away from Dilly Knox in the cottage. Turing and Knox both worked very well together, and both being ex "King's men", ie. of the Cambridge College they both attended, they felt some comradeship. However, the ambitious Turing wanted a project of his very own to get his teeth into.

Hut 8 was built in 1940, and it was to be the home of naval code-breakers. Decrypts of German naval Enigma messages were sent onto the naval intelligence Section in Hut 4, and then passed on as Z material, to the Admiralty, which in turn forwarded intelligence to the fleets at sea. When the Hut 8 section moved into the brick-built Block D, on 19th February 1943, the original wooden Hut 8 building was renamed Hut 18, and used for other purposes.

In 1940, Turing took charge of Hut 8 naval code-breaking and hired a second-in-command, Hugh Alexander.

Before he and his team could begin deeper work on the naval Enigma system, Turing needed further clues and information as to its inner workings. It couldn't be solved by mathematics and statistics alone. So with the help of the Royal Navy, a plan was devised to attack a soft target just to "pinch", i.e. Steal, a complete set of Enigma rotors (since each rotor had a different wiring configuration), as well as daily setting sheets and code-books. In response to this, the Royal Navy attacked several German weather ships, which were disguised as Norwegian trawlers, and only lightly armed. These trawlers were sending weather reports back for the *Luftwaffe* and surface shipping, therefore they had several different code-books and rotor wheels on board. They were based in the north of the Atlantic, and in the Norwegian Sea. It is surprising that the Germans never knew what we were up to, since we attacked many of these weather ships. If they had found out that their systems were being compromised, they would simply have changed them.

Using the information recovered and by applying mathematical algorithms, Turing and his team started to break German naval Enigma, and forwarded everything on to the Admiralty via Hut 4, Intelligence Section. U-boats, which were being a menace to our merchant shipping, could now be tracked down, located and destroyed. Turing and his teams in Hut 8 were truly saving lives from this point.

Alan Turing was also quite an eccentric in many ways. He lived at the Crown Inn at Shenley, a hamlet about three miles north of Bletchley Park. Nowadays the Crown is a row of private houses, and Shenley has been integrated into the new city of Milton Keynes. Turing suffered from hay fever, and to overcome this problem he would wear his gas mask as he cycled to and from Bletchley Park every day in the summer. This frightened the life out of any locals who saw him, since fears about gas attacks were very real. Turing's bicycle had a broken cog, and this would regularly cause the chain to come off. To avoid this happening he worked out that he could peddle fifteen times forward and five back, to keep the chain in place.

Turing was also always concerned that if the Germans were to invade Britain, they would confiscate all his money. So he decided to convert all his wealth into silver ingots and he buried them between Bletchley Park and Shenley. He made a note of the exact geographical location of the burial spot, and put this information into a code to avoid anyone else finding it. After the war, he returned to dig up his silver bullion to discover that he could not break his own code. So, with the assistance of one of his colleagues from Bletchley Park, and a crude metal detector made from a minesweeper, they tried but failed to locate the silver. If you visit Bletchley Park today please refrain from bringing a bucket and spade with you, as the silver is possibly underneath one of the many new housing estates in Milton Keynes.

During his time at Bletchley, Turing decided to join the Home Guard, known as the "local defence volunteers", and sometimes referred to as "Dad's Army". However, to join the Home Guard is still to sign-up to the army. Turing only joined so that he could fulfil his wish to learn how to fire a rifle, and with that achieved, he simply decided not to turn up anymore. This made him officially "absent-without-leave" (AWOL), or a deserter. As a result, the police were looking for him. This caused a lot of red faces at Bletchley Park, who were obliged to give some kind of explanation for his absence from the army, without breathing a word of the top-secret work they were involved with. It was also established that he intentionally made errors on his initial application, so it was all completely invalid and the whole incident was brushed under the carpet.

It is well known nowadays that Alan Turing was a homosexual, so we could well ask the question: why on earth did he propose marriage to one of his female colleagues, Joan Clark? After a few months, he admitted to Joan that he was a homosexual and their relationship could never work. Joan maintained that she had known all along but that their union could still be useful for them both. Turing told her that he would never be able to have a full relationship with her, and eventually broke off the engagement.

Work continued at Hut 8, and Alan Turing and the team were breaking into naval Enigma on a regular basis. Of course, there were always gaps whenever a code-book was changed, and the team sweated until an up-to-date code-book could be recovered. Life was good at Bletchley Park: green grass, no Blitz, no rationing, and plenty of entertainment, work hard, play hard and a night out in London was quite easy with the main-line train station just around the corner. And best of all, the United States were now our allies in the war.

All hopes and moods changed at Bletchley Park on the 1st February 1942. All of a sudden, we could no longer read the U-boat codes. This was a massive blow for the allied war effort, Hitler's U-boats were decimating our merchant fleets, the Germans even called it "Happy time. During the next nine months the Allies lost 5.4 million tonnes of merchant shipping owing to the successes of the U-boats and Bletchley Park: not being able to read the codes. (*Story of the recovery appears in an earlier chapter*).

Meanwhile, Turing travelled to the USA and Hugh Alexander became head of Hut 8. In November 1942, Alan Turing disembarked the Cunard liner Queen Elizabeth in New York. After some issues with immigration Turing went to the National Cash Register Company in Ohio. He was to oversee the designs of the high-speed Bombe machines that NCR were building. The staff at NCR had no idea that Turing was a code-breaker but realised he must be someone rather special due to the VIPs who accompanied him. One of the staff that Turing was working with asked for help to solve a puzzle in a daily newspaper, possibly to try to ascertain if he was a code-breaker. Turing replied "oh no, I am sorry. I can never solve those problems in the Herald and Tribune."

Turing also visited the Bell Telephone Company to assist with the manufacture of a safe voice encipher machine (scrambler), for Roosevelt to eventually use to speak confidentially to Churchill via the transatlantic telephone line. In March 1943, Turing returned to Britain, and was no longer head of Hut 8, he became a general consultant or Trouble Shooter if you like. But Turing was always known as, and called "the prof" Hut 8 had been relocated in early 1943 into a new brick-built Block D, and the department kept its classification as Hut 8. The original Hut 8 was renumbered Hut 18. All the huts at Bletchley Park were renumbered as departments moved around. Huts and brick blocks were always called by their original building numbers rather than being called a particular department, so as to give no clue as to their actual function, for security reasons. Sometimes they were even named after the heads of the department.

One of the pressing issues at Bletchley Park was how to break a code called Tunney. Tunney was known as a Fish code. Fish is what Bletchley Park called non-Morse traffic. This was a teleprinter-based transmission from a machine called Lorenz. Bletchley Park staff had no idea of the actual German name of the machine so they named all non-Morse teleprinter transmissions after fish. Tunny (*tuna fish*) was the name of the signal enciphered by the Lorenz SZ40/42. This machine was used by Hitler himself to send battle plans and high-grade traffic to his generals. The code had already been broken due to a German operator making a terrible blunder which is explained in a later chapter. The code was being broken by hand but taking far too long. Max Newman, one of Turing's former lecturers from his days at Cambridge, was now working at Bletchley Park. He had his own department there called the Newmanry at Block H. Newman and his team were struggling, trying to mechanise the Tunny code-breaking effort but having many problems with machines failing.

In 1943, Turing visited his former lecturer at the Newmanry and was shown the problem. Turing studied Bill Tutte's amazing work where Tutte reconstructed the internal workings of the Lorenz machine *(Lorenz to Colossus chapter),* Turing came up with an answer to part of the issue which became named "Turingismus" He later explained to Newman that he knew a brilliant engineer who was using thermionic valves *(radio valves or U.S. vacuum tubes)* for high-speed switching circuits to increase the efficiency of trunk telephone dialling at the Post Office Research Station at Dollis Hill, North London. Alan Turing did not become the chief figure in the Tunny work, and in particular did not design or build "Colossus", the world's first electronic digital computer *(installed at Bletchley park)* but he did direct Newman to Tommy Flowers with whom Turing had had dealings with at Dollis Hill. Alan Turing left Bletchley Park in June 1944, effectively transferring himself to Hanslope Park.

Life after Bletchley Park
Following Turing's work at the Bell laboratories in the US, he pursued the idea of electronic enciphering of speech in the telephone system. In the latter part of the war, he moved to work for the MI6 Radio Security Service (*now HMFCO Foreign & Commonwealth Office*) at Hanslope Park Buckinghamshire, ten miles north of Bletchley. There he further developed his knowledge of electronics with the assistance of engineer Donald Bayley. Together they undertook the design and construction of a portable secure voice communications machine code-named "Dahlia". Donald Bailey was a young engineer who later recalled how Turing's workshop skills left much to be desired, as when Turing was in the workshop he often heard him shout "Ouch!, Ouch!" as he invariably burnt his fingers on his soldering iron, and gave himself electric shocks as he tended to work with the current switched on.

Turing was always very open about his sexuality. Even at Bletchley Park an eye was kept on him, since his predilections clearly carried a risk of leading him into behaviour which was then illegal. This could have been a massive security risk if Turing was to become blackmailed, or even kidnapped, since he was privy to highly confidential government information. At one stage it risked being reported to Sir Stewart Menzies, the Chief of MI6, which would probably have resulted with Turing being sacked. This would have been a disaster for Britain considering Turing's value as the government's top code-breaker. But Turing's behaviour remained open, including discussing it with Donald Bailey at Hanslope Park. Turing went on foreign holidays to Scandinavia with homosexual groups, as well as taking a "gay" holiday in Greece. This obviously caused concern with MI6 and the American equivalent N.S.A. (National Security Agency) as he was still working for them, unbeknown to any of his work colleagues. The security services were becoming concerned with Turing's out-of-work activities, especially with the impending cold war with Russia.

Alan Turing completed his work on the Dahlia voice scrambler; it worked perfectly but unfortunately was never used.

TICOM

As the war in Europe came to a conclusion in May 1945, an American-led organisation "Target Information Committee" (TICOM) was set up to get to as many German communication locations as quickly as possible before the Russians. Once the Ticom team was there, they were to remove and bring back to Britain as much equipment as possible, including radio equipment and cipher machinery. It was considered possible that if the Russians obtained some of the advanced German communications equipment they may use it, and if they did we would have the knowledge to compromise their communications. This had never been confirmed by the security services. However Alan Turing became part of one of the TICOM teams. He was flown to France, met up with an American transport section and travelled across many of the European battlefields.

He was able to identify the equipment, and it was loaded onto trucks to be brought back to Britain. The team also found machinery that had never seen before but Turing had a hunch that it was connected the cipher he was attempting to break just a year before (possibly Lorenz SZ40/42 or Siemens T52 *Geheimfernschreiber*, "secret writer"). There were even German radio operators who pleaded to be taken prisoner before the Russians found them. At least three truck-loads along with the German operators. Came to a secret locations in Britain, one was possibly Whaddon Hall a Special Communication Unit of MI6 section VIII. In Buckinghamshire. Much of this equipment is now owned by GCHQ and some of it is on loan and displayed at Bletchley Park museum.

ACE

By late 1945 Turing started work at the National Physical Laboratory (*NPL*) in Teddington, Middlesex. There, he worked on the world's first computer, using the stored program concept. He was employed by the Department of Science & Industrial Research, which was part of the Civil Service, and the computer was called ACE (Automatic Computing Engine). This project became very frustrating for Turing since he found the department infuriatingly inefficient. He was no longer at Bletchley Park in a situation of war, where he needed only to click his fingers to get what he wanted. In the Civil Service (DSIR) everything was run by committee, all components have to be ordered in triplicate. There were times when the wrong components would be delivered, and the right ones had gone somewhere else. Delays and more delays. A newspaper article read "Dr. Turing's Electronic Brain ACE is over budget and will be obsolete before it is completed." Turing became increasingly frustrated and left for a sabbatical, ending up back at Cambridge.

At Cambridge Turing continued yet more research into obscure mathematical theories. Then, one day, he was contacted by his old friend and colleague Max Newman. Newman offered Turing a job at Manchester University where they were building the world's first fully-programmable computer, known as the "Manchester 1" an extension of the "The Baby" which was the world's first stored program computer built in 1948 at Manchester University.

Newman was so keen to get Turing into his department, that he initially offered Turing a job as Reader in the Mathematics department. Even though his salary was going to be less at Manchester than at the DS&IR, he was very pleased to get away from the Civil Service. So he resigned from the NPL and moved to Wilmslow in Cheshire, and in 1948 started work at Manchester University.

In 1949 he became the deputy director of the Computing laboratory (there was no director). Turing was starting to look at Artificial Intelligence, as well as working on software for the new computer, which was basically the Turing universal machine. In October 1950 in the quarterly publication "Mind", Turing asked his profound question "Can machines think?" He proposed a test that could establish whether a person is talking to a computer or a human being. This became known as the Turing Test. You have probably used a form of this test yourself. It is commonly found on the Internet in the form of "CAPTCHA". The computer will generate random images that a human will recognise as letters or numbers. If you can recognise these from the image, and type them in correctly, you pass the test as human and the host will allow you access. Turing's original procedure was a series of questions and answers. Depending on the answer to other party would establish whether you are a computer or human being. Turing called this procedure the imitation game.

Unbeknown to his colleagues at Manchester, Turing was still involved with work for the Security Services. He was now also being followed by security agents as he travelled on foreign escapades with the homosexual fraternity. Meanwhile, Turing was working on yet another venture. The

72

Fibonacci sequence is a special order of numbers that appears commonly in nature. Next time that you observe a sunflower, seedpod or pine cone you will note the geometric pattern of the seeds. This pattern is caused by a Fibonacci sequence of numbers, and connects mathematics to the natural world. Turing's endless fascination with, and research into, a wide-range of fields, is impressive and shouldn't be overlooked.

Turing also looked into animal skin patterns and their mathematical connections, a subject now known as morphogenesis *(from the Greek morphê shape and genesis creation, literally, "beginning of the shape")*. This led his research into the reproduction of neurological cells in the brain and how they communicate with the central nervous system. For his work in this field Alan Turing became a Fellow of the Royal Society (FRS), and he also obtained an OBE for his war work. In 1951, Turing was at the top of his profession, and it seemed that things could not get better for him.   Then!

All came tumbling down

Early in January 1952, Turing, then aged 39, started a relationship with Arnold Murray, a 19-year-old unemployed man. Turing met Murray just before the previous Christmas outside the Regal Cinema when walking down Manchester's Oxford Road. On leaving the theatre he happened to meet Murray and got chatting. After a drink in the local pub Turing invited his new friend to his house for a meal, a relationship was struck up and Murray moved in with Turing. A fortnight later they had a big row over some missing cash and as a result Murray walked out or was thrown out. On 23rd January Turing's house was burgled. Murray told Turing that the burglar was an acquaintance of his and Turing reported the crime to the police. During the investigation he acknowledged a sexual relationship with Murray. Homosexual acts were criminal offences in the United Kingdom at that time and both men were charged with gross indecency under Section 11 of the Criminal Law Amendment Act 1885.

Alan Turing appeared at the Cheshire quarterly sessions at Knutsford on 31st March 1952. Two of his character witnesses were his friends and colleagues Hugh Alexander, who had taken over from Turing at Bletchley Park and was now working at GCHQ and Max Newman, now the head of the computing research Department at Manchester University. They spoke of Alan Turing's important work during World War II although there was obviously no mention of what he actually did, as well as his new scientific research at Manchester University.

Turing entered a plea of "guilty", in spite of the fact that he felt no remorse or guilt for having committed acts of homosexuality. The case, Regina v. Turing and Murray, was brought to trial on 31ˢᵗ March 1952. Turing was convicted and given a choice between imprisonment and probation, which would be conditional on his agreement to undergo hormonal treatment designed to reduce libido. He accepted the option of treatment via injections of Stilboestrol, a synthetic oestrogen. This treatment was continued for the course of one year, and it rendered Turing impotent and caused him to grow breasts. Turing's prediction that "no doubt I shall emerge from it all a different man, but quite who I've not found out" seemed horribly prescient. Murray, meanwhile, was given a conditional discharge

The whole story got into the newspapers and Turing's conviction led to the removal of his security clearance, and he was barred from continuing with his secret work for the Government Communications Headquarters (GCHQ), the British signals intelligence agency that had evolved from GC&CS at Bletchley Park in 1946 (though he kept his academic job). He was denied entry into the United States after his conviction in 1952, but was free to visit other European countries, even though this was viewed by some as a security risk. At the time, there was acute public anxiety about homosexual entrapment of spies by Soviet agents, because of the recent exposure of the first two members of the Cambridge Five, Guy Burgess and Donald Maclean, as KGB double agents. Turing was never accused of espionage, but in common with all who had worked at Bletchley Park, he was prevented by the Official Secrets Act from discussing his war work

Turing continued his work into morphogenesis but started to become depressed. He sought advice from a psychiatrist and he started to notice some very strange side-effects from his oestrogen injections. He became more depressed as time went on and eventually he wrote a note to his psychiatrist. "Turing believes machines think. Turing lies with men. Therefore machines do not think".

Events just prior to his 42nd birthday:
Monday 7 June 1954 was a bank holiday. It is believed that Turing finished replying to some invitations and went to his makeshift laboratory in a spare room in his house to complete some experimental work. He then went to bed taking an apple with him, something he often did.

Tuesday 8 June 1954
In the morning Turing's housekeeper arrived at his home "Holymeade" in Wilmslow Cheshire. She found some of the house lights on, and the curtains still drawn. When she went upstairs, she found Alan Turing in bed with a half-eaten apple by his side. He was dead.

Wednesday 9th June 1954
An autopsy was performed, and concluded that he had died from cyanide poisoning.

Thursday, 10 June 1954
An inquest was heard. The verdict was suicide.

Friday 11th of June 1954 Turing's body was taken to Woking in Surrey, close to where his mother then lived.

Saturday, 12 June 1954
Alan Turing was cremated at Woking crematorium.

His mother said that Alan would never have committed suicide. She believed that he was probably performing some strange experiments using dangerous chemicals. "Alan never washed his hands," she said.

There have always been questions asked over his death. Many years later, in the 1980s, the wartime operations of Bletchley Park were starting to be released by the government, and the importance of the work which Alan Turing did for his country began to be realised. There is an exhibition of his work in the museum at Bletchley Park, with many of his papers on mathematics on display. At Manchester University, where he did so much of his research, there is a statue and a building named after him. His house Holymeade, in Wilmslow, as well as his birthplace in Warrington Crescent, West London (now the Colonnades Hotel), bear blue plaques commemorating the life of Alan Turing. On 24th December 2013, sixty-two years after his conviction, Alan Turing was granted a royal pardon by her Majesty Queen Elizabeth II.

There is just one last question. Many people believe that the logo for the Apple Corporation was a tribute to Alan Turing. With the rainbow colours an obvious nod to the gay community, and the bite out of the Apple representing Alan Turing's deadly bite. Shortly before his premature death on 5th October 2011 (aged 56), Steve Jobs, the co-founder, Chairman and CEO of Apple Incorporated, was asked the question "Does the Apple logo represent Alan Turing's Apple?" Steve Jobs replied, "No it doesn't but I wish to God it did."

Nowadays there are many publications that represent the work of Alan Turing. You can even buy an Alan Turing Monopoly game, exclusively sold by Bletchley Park. There is an excellent play by Hugh Whitmore called "Breaking the code" Which tells of Turing's life. I have even come across an Alan Turing Lego man and finally the 2014 film release of The Imitation Game is also believed to be an authoritative dramatisation of Turing's life (*which has all the right facts but not necessarily the right order*).

We will probably never know the full circumstances surrounding Alan Turing's death. There are so many conspiracy theories owing to his continued work with the security services. As far as we're concerned and until proven otherwise, he committed suicide. But there is one thing we can be certain of. Every time you switch on your computer, your laptop, iPad, or even open a Word document or an Excel file, you are using the stored program concept. Your device was built Turing-compatible and you are using the basic computer architecture devised by Alan Turing in the 1930s.

The question is: Was Alan Mathison Turing Ph.D. FRS "Father of Theoretical Computer Science and Artificial Intelligence" the man who possibly knew just a bit too much?

So Who Broke the Enigma Code Anyway?

With the conclusion of World War II in August 1945, Bletchley Park closed down as a War Station. Papers were burnt, machinery dismantled and by April 1946 Barbara Abernethy, personal assistant to the head of the GC&CS returned the keys to her superiors in London. The Staff who worked at Bletchley Park returned to civilian life, many in the world of academia, completing university degrees. Others went to the new Government Communication Headquarters, initially at Eastcote in Middlesex and then onto Cheltenham as it remains to this day. Some of the big brains went on to Manchester University to invent the worlds' first fully programmable computers. Bletchley Park became the home for the General Post Office (GPO later BT) Telephone engineering Training School also, the Civil Aviation Authority, later a Teachers Training College was set up at Bletchley Park. But, one thing was for sure, nobody knew what went on there during World War II. During the 1980's the GPO along with other organisations moved away to new locations. The whole of Bletchley Park site was part owned by British Telecomm (BT) and partly by the Government.

Now for the second time in the life of Bletchley Park demolition hung over its head likened to the Sword of Damocles. This time the plan was not for a housing estate as in Captain Faulkner's day of 1937, this time the destruction would make way for a major Supermarket's distribution Depot. BT had already started to demolish many of the wartime buildings. The problem was that no one knew of the full historical significance of the site. In 1974 Captain Frederick Winterbotham's book was published, "The Ultra Secret", this was the first British book to tell the story of Bletchley Park's work during World War II The media were beginning to cotton on as to the important role that Bletchley Park had during the War. Now the stories were out, programs were being made, articles were being written and some of the Veterans were coming forward with their stories. But, most importantly, a group of dedicated people came forward and realised that BT's destruction of the Bletchley Park site was tantamount to vandalism. These buildings were of historical significance in British History. The best way to stop the demolition would be to apply for the buildings to become listed, but the time factor was too great.   One member of the group suggested listing all the trees on the site.   Being a Park, there were many hundreds of beautiful rare trees a pursuit from one of the original owners Sir Herbert Samuel Leon.

. The then Borough of Milton Keynes acted very swiftly to the application, very soon tree preservation orders were in place.   As soon as the trees were listed, the plan for leveling the site could not proceed.   Eventually English Heritage listed all the Buildings to Grade II.   In 1992 there was the inaugural meeting at King's College, London, where The Bletchley Park Trust was formed. With all the publicity surrounding Bletchley Park, along with the Government releasing many documents, a deal was eventually agreed with a lease for 250 years for Bletchley Park to become a permanent museum as the Home of the World War II code-breakers.   With years of hard work from many volunteers, Bletchley Park has now become a world class museum. Together with lottery funding, many of the buildings have been returned to their original form.   Inside the buildings are exhibitions and demonstrations of code- breaking machinery.   There are also special event days: Wartime Transport as in cars and buses.   1940's fashion shows reflecting wartime styles.   In the early days of the Bletchley Park Museum a special event was held, an unveiling of a memorial to commemorate the work and amazing achievements of the Polish code-breakers during the leading up to WWII.

"So who did break the Enigma Code anyway?"
        During World War 1 the Admiralty was responsible for the majority of code-Breaking with department NID25 based in room 40 at the Old Admiralty Buildings. The War Office also had a small code-breaking facility known as MI1B. In 1919 these two organisations were brought under one roof. Eventually to become The Government "Code and Cipher School" GC&CS based at Broadway Buildings Westminster. At the end of World War 1 Winston Churchill was the Secretary of State for War and Air. In 1923 Churchill published his book "World in Crisis 1911-1918".   Within the pages of this book, Churchill surprisingly admits to our code-breaking efforts.   He claimed that one of the reasons we were able to win the war in 1918 was due to our ability to read German Codes and act upon the information. During the 1920's, Germany became completely demoralised. Apart from losing the war, they also

lost their empire around the world together with territories in Europe and having also to pay reparations of 132 billion gold marks due to the Treaty of Versailles. The Treaty of Versailles was designed to prevent Germany from ever going to war again. Now also having the added humiliation of knowing their communications were being intercepted and read throughout the war. In the 1919 Treaty, Germany was allowed to have, with many restrictions, an army with no more than 100,000 troops. Mainly to have a defensive role, the Military was called the *Reichswehr* (Empire Defense). Erich Fellgiebel, Chief Communications Officer in the *Reichswehr* got to hear about Churchill's claim of reading codes. Fellgiebel stated that if Germany was ever in another conflict, they would never allow their codes to be read again. From then on Felligiebel was on the lookout for a completely secure cipher system. In the First World War code-books were used. These consisted of lists of words and corresponding codes. You would change your plain message to a totally meaningless jumble of words. These messages were normally sent by standard Morse code. The receiving station would then use their code-book to de-code the message. The code-breakers had methods of breaking the codes, sometimes with a captured code-book, then other times just working it out by a hand method. There were some other code- devices available. The One Time Pad, the Playfair Cipher, and Creaser transposition codes and there were also some gadgets with drums of moving letters, normally hand held.

Enigma

In 1915 two Dutch Marine Engineers Spengler and Van Hegel invented a machine using rotors to encipher messages. This idea was sold to Hugo Kotch another Dutchman who improved the design and sold the Patent to a German Engineering Company Sherbius & Ritter in 1919. Then Arthur Sherbius once again improved his machine into a saleable item. He gave the machine a name, a Greek word for an unsolvable puzzle, "Enigma". The machine was designed for the commercial markets. The idea was to sell it to international banks and finance houses to transmit confidential information by telegraph. These early Enigma machines were very bulky and heavy. They did not sell very well. Sherbius took his Enigma to the United States in 1921 but alas, it did not sell there either. In 1924 he brought the Enigma to England. Sherbius applied for and was granted a patent in London for his Enigma

79

machine then took the machine to the War Office to attempt to sell it as a military cipher machine. But once again, he was turned down, being told it was too slow and too easy to break into. This was one of the early cumbersome bulky machines, so Sherbius took his Enigma machine plans back to Germany and they made modifications to the machine. The Enigma machine was then redesigned to be made smaller, they then changed the complicated printing mechanism with a battery powered lamp board.   Now the Enigma is much smaller and compact and weighed 12 Kilos. The machine has now become a more saleable item. They started selling some Enigma's to embassies also to the Spanish government for military use. Sherbius then approaches the German military the *Reichswehr*.   He is put in touch with the head of *Reichswehr* Communications, Major Erich Fellgiebel.

After reviewing the machine and requesting modifications, Fellgiebel realises that this is exactly what he had been looking for, a cipher machine with such complexities and so easy to use, more important impossible to break into (it almost was)   A deal is done to supply the *Reichwehr* with the Enigma machine. The first machines went to the navy in 1926 and to then the army in 1928.   In 1935 the German military under Adolf Hitler became the *Wehrmacht*. The German Airforce, *Luftwaffe* also took on the Enigma.   During World War II it has been said that there were in excess of 70,000 Enigma machines in operational use on almost 200 networks.

Polish connection

In 1918 with the conclusion of World War 1 Poland was free for the first time in 123 years of Prussian the German Rule. But within months Poland was at war again. In 1919 Russia invaded Poland. In 1920 the battle for Warsaw takes place.   Warsaw is held from the Russian army by Marshall Pilsudski, the question is "How"? The Polish army was intercepting Russian Radio Transmissions. One of the Polish communications Officers "Jan Kawalewski" had instructions to intercept Russian radio signals and pass them on as soon as they were received. He was also told not to worry about the coded messages, just to concentrate on the plain text.   The shifts were long and boring, so to pass the time Kawalewksi took it upon himself to attempt and successfully de-cipher many of the coded Russian signals.   He became quite good at it. His messages were passed promptly to the generals of the cavalry.

Through this strategic intelligence gained, Marshall Pilsudski against all odds managed to defeat the Russians. After the war Pilsudski initiated the Polish Cipher Bureau. (*Biuro Szyfrów*). Colonel Gwido Langer, Head of Military Communications would take charge. Major Maximillian Ciezki would become Head of the German Section Department BS4. To engage more staff for this operation, a course was set up by Antoni Palluth, an engineer and lecturer at the Poznan University in Warsaw. Known then as the Adam Mickiewicz University in Poznań. The candidates for the course were mainly students of the mathematics department. At the end of the course three students excelled, Marian Rejewski Henryk Zygalski and Jersy Rozycki. In 1927 a communications and cipher department was set up in the basement of an army post in Warsaw. The code-breakers started to intercept German signals. Up to now the code-breakers had never seen an Enigma machine. At around the same time at Okecie Airport South of Warsaw, the Customs intercepted a large package being returned from the German Embassy back to Germany. The customs officers carefully unpacked it and photographed it, then put it back in the box and sent it on its way. This was a diplomatic Enigma Machine that would have come in very handy for our Polish code-breakers. It appears they may have at least obtained the photographs.

German Situation

Due to the conditions of the Treaty of Versailles, Germany was is in a desperate state. Inflation is running at a critical level. To buy one US Dollar in 1923 would have cost you 4.2 million, million Marks. Money became worthless, companies were going broke all the time and banks crashed. This anecdote is about a German business man who went broke in the late 1920s: His company made umbrellas and handbags. His name was Hans Thilo Schmidt. On the face of it he was a family man, married with children. However, Schmidt had a dark side to him. He would gamble, he liked a drink, he frequented night clubs. He certainly enjoyed other women, especially his own housemaid. To do all these things you need money. Thilo Schmidt had no money. Owing to his business failing he never had a job either. Now Hans had a brother, Rudolph, he had a job. Rudloph Thilo Schmidt was a general in the German Army. In fact he was one of the chiefs of the Berlin Cipher Bureau a very respected and high ranking position.

81

The Berlin Cipher Bureau is the planning centre for everything to do with the Enigma System. Rudolph had a soft spot for his brother, realising he was in a predicament, he offered him a job in the Cipher Bureau as a civilian assistant. This was a very low paid position. Hans took the job but he considered it below his station as he was unable to maintain his lifestyle. One day he was wondering how he could increase his income and he had a thought, "I wonder if I could sell some of these plans and documents of this Enigma system?". The next day he presented himself to the French Embassy in Berlin. He asked to be put in touch with an agent. Very cautiously the Embassy Staff took his details. He asked the officials to be discreet, as he knew what would happen to him if he was seen in the vicinity of the embassy. He was asked to return at a later date to give the embassy officials time to make the appropriate checks. On his return to the Embassy he was informed to make contact at a secret location at a hotel in Viviers, a town on the German/Belgium border. There he was to meet Rudolph Lemoine (real name Rudolf Stallman) code-name Rex. Hans Thilo Schmidt was also given a code-name Asche. The meeting took place in November 1931. Lemoine "Rex" who it has been said lived like a king, hence the code name. He worked for the Deuxieme bureau, the French intelligence organisation led by Captain Gustav Bertrand.

Secret Meeting

Lemoine laid the law down to Schmidt. He made it crystal clear that he would not stand for any nonsense, so therefore, what he had to sell had to be good. Thilo Schmidt showed the documents and plans he had borrowed from the Cipher Bureau. Lemoine took them to his room and photographed them. He made a generous payment to Thilo Schmidt. This scenario repeated itself throughout the 1930's. Thilo Schmidt was paid a fortune by the French. It is a miracle or stupidity that the Germans failed to notice that a minor member of staff at their top secret Cipher Bureau had suddenly entered the high life and was up to his old tricks with wine, women and song. However, the French intelligence organisation never had the setup to deal with this information. So they contacted the British secret service to try and sell this information, alas the British were not interested and turned the offer down.

This could have been one of the greatest blunders by our Intelligence services of all times. The French were also in league with the Polish Cipher

Bureau in Warsaw who had been working on the breaking of the Enigma for some time and therefore more than happy to accept the plans, documents, code-books along with training manuals of the German military Enigma machine (M3). However, just prior to receiving all the goodies from Germany, Marian Rejewski one of the polish protégé mathematicians amazingly using pure statistical mathematics reconstructed the internal structure and connections of the German military Enigma machine.

Another bit of an Enigma

In 1919 Arthur Sherbius invented a commercial machine it was heavy, bulky with a typewritten output. During the 1920's the machine was greatly reduced in size and now weighted approximately twelve kilograms. The output was now a lamp board using a four and a half volt battery power. Several Embassies purchased the Enigma cipher machine. The Enigma machine was used in the Spanish civil war. When the Germans took Enigma on board the *Reichwehr* made changes to the system. The rotor wheels were to have a completely different wiring configuration to the Enigmas on the open market.

Later the Germans introduced a modification that was a panel of connections that could be changed. There were ten connection cables changing the letters before the current even got to the rotor wheels. This was known as the *'Stecker brett'* or plug board. The setting for this and the rotors were changed daily using setting sheets. The rotors would come out of the Enigma every day and put back in a different order, as each rotor had a different wiring configuration. Later the Germans issued a selection of three rotors from a box of five. The German navy (*Kriegsmarine*) had eight different rotors, so their choice would be three out of eight giving the naval Enigma many more possibilities to break. Further naval security later on in the war was to issue new machines with a fourth rotor inside the Enigma machine (February 1941).

Another security feature to add complexity was the 'officer key' *(Offizier Schlüssel)*. In December 1932 at the Polish Cipher Bureau BS4 in their new home in the Saxon Palace in Warsaw, is where the German military Enigma (M3) was broken into for the first time. Though the information from the German agent Hans Thilo Schmidt was certainly of great assistance to the code-breakers and cannot be under-estimated, the fact was that the main work involved for the break came from Rejewski's sheer genius using advanced mathematics.

Antoni Palluth

He was an engineer and lecturer at Warsaw Polytechnic University. In the 1930's Palluth was one of the four Directors of the AVA Radio Company in Warsaw. On the face of it, they built military radio equipment but in a secret room in the factory they would build cryptographic machinery from the plans obtained from Thilo Schmidt, along with Rejewski's Research. The AVA Company built two cloned Enigma Machines. Then in 1933 a further fifteen Enigmas were constructed which were used by the Polish code-breakers throughout the 1930's to break the German Army and from 1935 its Air force (*Luftwaffe*) Enigma. The AVA Company produced a further two machines, one was called a Cyclometer, devised in the mid-1930s by Rejewski to catalog the cycle structure of Enigma permutations. The other machine was called the Bomba and would represent six Enigmas which would be used to work out the initial setup of the Enigma Rotors at the start of an intercepted message.

We are frequently asked why is the machine called a Bomba? A name that was also used later in Britain then the US with Alan Turing's cryptanalytic Bombe Machine. The story is that the engineers who were discussing the plans for the Bomba, were in a cafe in Warsaw eating Bomba Ice Creams at the time??!! I cannot imagine plans of a secret nature such as this being openly discussed in a café. The more credible explanation is that as the machine operated the sound of the contacts clicking internally probably sounded like a time bomb or Bomba in polish In 1938 Henry Zygalski developed a system of punched card sheets. 51 x 51 grid that he used as a manual device to find the Enigma message settings. The punched cards would be stacked in a pile of twenty six then they would be placed over a light box. The light would shine through the selected punched hole to reveal the Enigma settings. In 1937 Section BS4 code-breaking division moved to a new safe and secure camouflaged location in the Kabaty Woods near Pyry, South of Warsaw, and code-named "WICHER".

The First Meeting

Captain Gustav Bertrand set up a meeting with the Poles and the British in January 1939 which was attended by Alistair Denniston, Head at the Government Code and Cipher School and his Senior Code-Breaker Dilly Knox (Alfred Dillwyn Knox). The Poles were very suspicious of the British since the Munich Agreement of September 1938. They were worried that the British may come to some deal with the Germans after Neville Chamberlain's "Peace for our time" speech. Also present at the meetings were John Tiltman, army code-breaking Head at GC&CS and Hugh Foss Linguist and code-breaker GC&CS. The Poles were not going to give much away if anything. Dilly Knox was fuming as he claimed the whole affair at this meeting was a complete waste of time. He claimed the Poles knew no more than we did. He was wrong, they knew a lot more but they were not going to give the game away without some kind of guarantee that the British would help them if push came to shove with the Germans.

In March 1939 Prime Minister Neville Chamberlain signed` a document known as the "Anglo-Polish Military Pact" which guaranteed, should Germany invade Poland, Britain would come to their aid. Many people believed that this agreement would put pay to any future peace with Germany. The Polish code-breakers were throughout the 1930's intercepting and breaking German Army and Air-force (after 1935) Enigma. They did not and were not going to share that knowledge with the British. During mid-1939, the Polish code-breakers were reading German signals that indicated the German Military was massing on Polish borders. With this build up it was looking as if an invasion of Poland was very coming soon. It was now that the staff at BS4 had to act. It was obvious that should the Germans invade, and find the code-breakers secret headquarters, apart from torture and certain death, the work at BS4 would have been wasted. The code-breakers work had to be protected at all costs. In hindsight to loose Enigma, could have easily lost the war.

Second Meeting

Had Enigma had been compromised the Germans would simply change their systems, that would have been a disastrous situation, as a change like that could well stop anyone ever breaking Enigma again. Another meeting had to be hastily arranged with the assistance of Captain Bertrand and the M16 Paris Agent Alfred (Biffy) Dunderdale. The meeting was arranged and to be held at BS4 centre at Pyry. The Chief of M16 Stewart Menzies authorised the head of GC&CS Alistair Denniston along with his chief code-breaker Dilly Knox to travel to Pyry, They were joined later by the Royal Naval Commander Humphrey Sandwith, Head of Royal Navy's Y Service and Direction finding. At the meeting with the Polish code-breakers also present, was Bertrand's lead code-breaker Henri Braquenie. The meeting took place on the 26-28 July. To get there Denniston and Knox travelled through Germany for the last time. In Denniston's office at Bletchley Park Museum you will see Denniston's Passport Stamped with the mark of the Third Reich for the transit to this meeting just five weeks prior to the war. Dilly Knox, though very ill at the time with cancer, was in his typical bad mood thinking this is another waste of time as was the January meeting. Then Knox was to learn something so simple which he had been taxing his brain for months with. He could have kicked himself. He had been trying to work out the internal wiring from the Enigma keyboard and plug board to the entry wheel that made contact with the first rotor in the Enigma (fixed entry rotor), which is the on right hand side. He thought it may have been the QWERTY order, or even the QWERTZU (German) order. He tried many combinations. He knows that if he could not work this out we may never be able to break the German Military M3 Enigma.

At this stage Knox was not aware that the Poles had been breaking Enigma thought the 1930's. These connections were a real bugbear to him. Then out of the blue, Knox asked the Polish code-breakers "Have you actually ever broken the Enigma?" "Of course" they replied, when he discovered that they had, he enquired "what is the connection order to the entry wheel?" as he had tried every combination. To his absolute amazement the Poles advised him the order from the plug board to the entry rotor was ABCDE etc. Yes it was just alphabetical order all along!! The latter part of the meeting was then to arrange that BS4 at Pyry should close down as soon as possible. Staff would be evacuated to Paris, machinery and documents would be destroyed beyond recognition. Two Enigma machines would be spared. Bertrand initially took them back to Paris, then on the 16th August 1939 Bertram and Biffy Dunderdale M16 came to London. They stepped off the Golden Arrow Train at Victoria

Station, it was there that they met the Chief of MI6 Stewart Menzies waiting under the clock they handed over one of the cloned Enigma Machines that was built by the AVA Radio Company in Warsaw. This machine eventually came to Bletchley Park, it was this machine that Dilly Knox and his team used to break the Enigma M3 in the following January 1940. It needs to be noted that the Germans were continuingly implementing further security adaptations to the Enigma this kept the British code-breakers on their toes throughout the war.

Evacuation

Meanwhile the Polish code-breakers were on the move. 1st September 1939 Germany invaded Poland. The Polish code- breakers and engineers make their way to Paris. They flee Poland by the safest route, they head for Romania which at this time was a passive ally of Germany. They reached Bucharest where there are German *Abwehr* Officers on the lookout for Polish businessmen escaping Poland. The code-breakers made for the French Embassy to obtain the documentation they require to travel to Paris. The route took them from Bucharest by train via Yugoslavia and Italy. They arrived safely in Paris in October 1939 with the assistance of Bertrand. A code-breaking Centre was set up in the Chateau Vignolles near *Gretz Armainvilliers*, code-name "PC BRUNO". Bartrand was to head the facility for the rest of the war. Henri Braquenie now Bertrand's Second in Command, set up a secure teleprinter link to transmit information to Bletchley Park. To keep signals secure, they were encoded the messages using the AVA cloned Enigma machine. If messages were intercepted, to confuse the German Interceptors some messages would end with Heil Hitler! January 1940, Alan Turing visits the Bruno Centre, The main reasons for the visit was for an exchange of knowledge with Marian Rejewski to discuss the development of the first British Bombe Machine. Also to deliver some special stationery. We were supplying the French, Polish and now some Spanish code-breakers with special punched sheets on non-standard paper. These were made in Banbury Oxfordshire. The procedure became called "Bamberismus".

The British Bombe machine

Based on the theory of the Polish Bomba by Marian Rejewski. The British Bombe designed by Alan Turing who was assisted by Gordon

Welchman and Harold Keen of the British Tabulating Machinery Company of Letchworth Garden City, Hertfordshire. The principle of the machine was to simulate thirty six Enigma machines at high speed. The idea was to eliminate the vast potential of a 159 million million million (159^{18}) to leave just a handful of possibilities, then eventually work out the exact settings on that particular network for that day. The Germans had in excess of 180 military radio networks. Virtually each network would have its own set of code-books (Setting Sheets). Each Network's settings would change at zero hour GMT (Midnight for us), where ever that particular enemy unit was based, regardless of which time zone that they were operating in. Some units would even be ordered to change their settings twice a day. Bletchley Park was running a twenty four hour watch for any signals the happened to come in overnight on that new setting, to give the code-breakers maximum time for the prospect of an early break, as in this game time is the essence.

There were 211 Bombe Machines though just a few were at Bletchley, some even operated at requisitioned large country houses close by. The majority were located at out-stations at Stanmore and Eastcote north of London. They were operated by the Womens Royal Navy Services "Wrens". The machines were maintained by Royal air force Engineers. The results from the Bombe runs known as *Jobs Up!* where checked and teleprintered up to the Bombe control room close to Hut 3 at Bletchley Park.

Battle of France

In May 1940 all was to change for the BRUNO Centre as the Germans marched into France. They also changed some vital message settings to the M3 Enigma. The Germans also added a further two rotors. There now is a choice of three out of five different rotors, which badly set back the code-breakers. Once again, like Gypsies, it was time to move on. At midnight on 10th June 1940 all traces of BRUNO had disappeared as if they had never existed, just four days prior to the Germans capturing Paris. The code-breakers were to be temporarily transferred to French Algiers. Initially the Germans only invaded the north of France. The South was to remain French under a kind of German control, though the entire French Government transferred to the Spa Town of Vichy.

The control became steadily more German. Marshall Philippe Petain had been one of France's heroes from World War 1

Petain was made Premier of Vichy, France, but he collaborated with the Germans, by rounding up any resistance fighters and handing them over to the Gestapo. BRUNO set up and continued a small code-breaking department in Vichy while Bertrand searched for a new permanent home. Once again our Code-breakers are on the move. After some more temporary sites, on 1st October 1940 Captain Bertrand had been able to set up a clandestine business with forged documentation at the small town of Uzes near to Nimes. It was the cover for a new code-breaking centre with a new code-name "CADIX". The code-breakers all made for their new home at Les Fouzes Villa Uzes. A French manufacturer was able to make parts for four further cloned Enigma machines. An out station is set up by Bertrand in Algiers. There was a periodic exchange of staff with CADIX. Though the CADIX operation was very successful, living conditions were becoming intolerable. The heat, the mosquitoes, cockroaches etc. Decrypted information was re-encoded using the cloned Enigma Machines and sent by radio to England, picked up by intercept (Y) stations then passed to Bletchley Park. Doom and gloom set in as they receive information that the ship *Lamoricier* sinks in unclear circumstances, close to the Balearic Islands. Onboard were Jerzi Rozycki along with other Cipher Staff returning from the out station at the Chateau Couba on the outskirts of Algiers. On 11th November 1942 Marshall Petain capitulates with the Germans, this was the final straw for CADIX. The whole of France now comes under full German Control. Marshall Petain gives intelligence to the Germans so that they are able to round up even more of the resistance and eliminate them. The work at CADIX included the interception and code-breaking of enemy signals including transmitting them to Bletchley Park, the following information is an example of their work:

Location of Wehrmacht Command Posts
Activity of S S Agents (SD)
Operations of the *Luftwaffe* in Greece
Extermination camps in occupied Europe
Concentration Camps in Russia
The *Abwehr* German spy network

There are now massive German troop movements to the South of France heading towards Marseilles for transportation to North Africa to join Rommel's Africa Corps. German communications and direction finding units are now searching for clandestine radio transmissions and are homing in on the CADIX Operations. The Germans are now definitely on the case. As CADIX shuts down, again everything is destroyed all the evidence is removed, the staff scatter and made a run for it. One group decided to get to Switzerland which would involve a treacherous hike across the winter Pyrenees mountain range. They found a guide and paid him everything they could afford. The guide would be able to locate the roads and paths across the mountains. Gwido Langer Head of the Polish Section, Antoni Palluth Chief Engineer and Major Maksymilian Ciężki, expert in German amongst others were to head to Switzerland. Unfortunately, they were confronted by the S.S. as their guide betrayed them to the Germans. They were arrested and transported to Sachenhausen Concentration Camp in Oranienburg north of Berlin.

Marian Rejewski, Henryk Zygalski with three radio engineers, attempted to get to Britain. By the 29th January 1943 they crossed the Spanish Border. They were captured by the Spanish frontier Guards and put in several Spanish gaols. They were treated very badly. Spain was neutral in World War II but leaned very heavily towards the Germans. Spain was bursting with German agents working from the *Abwehr* (German Intelligence Service). The prisoners went on hunger strike. They made a kind of friendship with the prison Chaplin who contacted Polish Red Cross and with official complaints from the British Government. On 4th May 1943 after three months of incarceration, the Spanish authorities released the prisoners and issued them with appropriate documentation. The code-breakers and Engineers headed for Portugal. 22 July 1943 they made contact with the crew of a clandestine fishing boat on the Portuguese coast. They were then taken to a location where they met up with a British destroyer which transported them to the safety of Gibraltar. Once there, they were again transferred to an RAF aircraft that flew them to the Polish Army centre at Kinross in Scotland. Rejewski was soon transferred to Boxmore in Hertfordshire along with Henryk Zygaski. It was there that they worked on S.S. Hand Ciphers for the rest of the war. For reasons only known to British

Intelligence, they were never allowed to work on Enigma again or to know of the whereabouts of Bletchley Park.

HENRYK ZYGALSKI
Mathematician and code-breaker

After the war, he settled in Britain and became a Lecturer in Mathematics and Statistics at the University of Surrey – he died 30th August 1978.

MARION REJEWSKI
Mathematician and code-breaker

After the war, he returned to his family in Poland. Poland was then under Communist control the authorities would not allow Rejewski to work in any form of academia. He had several jobs working as an accountant and bookkeeper. He died 13th February 1980.

JERZY ROZYCKI
Mathematician and code-breaker

Returning from Algiers along with three radio engineers, their ship the *Lamoricier* sank in unclear circumstances on the 11th November 1942

ANTONI PALLUTH
Civil engineer and lecturer at Poznan University

He was betrayed by his Guide, Sent to Sachsenhausen Concentration Camp. Tortured but never divulged the secrets of Enigma. He died as the camp was attacked by an allied air raid 18th April 1944.

COLONEL GUIDO LANGER
Head of Polish code-breaking bs4

He was eventually captured escaping with others in France. Sent to Sachsenhausen concentration camp. Released in 1945 with severe malnutrition. Taken to the Polish Base in Kinross in Scotland where he died on 30th March 1948. In 2010 his body was exhumed and returned to Poland. He was then re-buried with full military honours.

MAJOR MAXSYMILIAM CIEZKI

Second in command BS4 and expert in German language. Captured and incarcerated at Sachsenhausen Concentration Camp. Released in 1945 with malnutrition. Came to England where he died 9th November 1951.

There were many others along with the above that worked at the BS4 Polish Cipher Bureau and then on to other locations. There were also French and Spanish code-breakers and engineers who experienced similar circumstances. Today we could only mention a few.

CAPTAIN GUSTAV BERTRAND
French military intelligence officer.

5th January 1944, at the Sacre Coeur in Paris, Bertrand was waiting to meet up with his courier from London, when he was arrested by the Germans. He pretended to yield to them giving them names of agents who were safely in hiding out of the Country. He was put under house arrest in Vichy with his wife. Pending the Germans believing he was going to work for them. On 2nd June 1944 he and his wife escaped by a Lysander Aircraft to Britain. After the war he went back to the French Secret Service. He retired in 1950 to become Mayor of Theoule-Sur-Mer in the South of France. In 1973 he wrote the first book telling the story of breaking the Enigma. The Paris publishing house Plon published his book, *Enigma ou la plus grande énigme de la guerre 1939-1945* ("Enigma or the Greatest Enigma of the War of 1939-1945") He died in 1976.

RUDLPH LEMOINE
(Alias Rudolph Stallman) code-name "REX"

A French Intelligence Agent who was arrested in Cologne in 1938 by the Gestapo. On information divulged to save his skin he betrayed his German Agent Hans Thilo Schmidt code-name "Asche". Rudolph Stallman died in 1946.

HANS THILO SCHMIDT
Code-name "ACSHE"

Arrested by the Gestapo on 1st April 1943. It is said he committed suicide in September 1943. His daughter was called to identify his body. She claims his suicide was forced.

RUDOLPH THILO SCHMIDT

He held a senior Position just below Field Marshall in the Berlin Cipher Bureau. He employed his brother who turned out to be a traitor. He was anti-Hitler and anti-Nazi he was arrested, court-martialed and sacked from his position. How on earth did he get away with that?? He died at the age of 70 in 1957.

WILFRED (BIFFY) DUNDERDALE

MI6 Agent in Paris. Set up liaison with MI6, GC&CS and the French Intelligence Bureau. MI6 Agent information is not normally available. We do however know that he died 13th November 1990 at the age of 98. "Biffy" as his prowess as a boxer in the Navy at the end of the First World War. He worked at the Paris British Embassy Passport Office as a cover (*Station 45000MI6*), working with the *Deuxieme* Bureau on the Soviet and German Section. This suave flamboyant agent was a good friend of Ian Fleming who worked for the British Admiralty in Intelligence at Room 39 of the Admiralty,. It has been suggested that Dunderdale could have been one of the models for James Bond.

So my questions remain.

"So who broke the Enigma Code anyway?"

It has been stated that the Polish code-breakers simply ran out of resources and time. After all, the procedures in use by the Poles, predictably was to change as it did in May 1940 and then every few months. The Germans were continually updating their security procedures. There was also a predicted change to the Enigma's indicating setup system. So it could be said, that it was the code-breakers at Bletchley Park who really broke the Enigma code as Enigma was continuing to evolve with the forever changing security procedures. Bletchley Park had resources, time and personnel as in the brilliant mathematicians who worked with Dilly Knox, such as Alan Turing, John Jeffries, Peter Twinn with Margaret Rock and Linguist Mavis Lever who all who worked in the cottage at Bletchley Park. In January 1940, Dilly Knox and his team made the first British break into the German Military Enigma, then subsequent breaks for the rest of the war.

But! There is a big BUT! If it wasn't for the incredible initial work carried out by Marian Rejewski, Henryk Zygalski, Jerzy Rozycki who made the mathematical calculations, along with Antoni Palluth and all the engineers that built cloned Enigmas, from photos and stolen plans, would we have even had the success we did?

After all the Poles were working under extreme pressure to do what they did, and to conduct that important meeting with the French and the British on 25th July 1939 when the Germans poised to smash down the doors of Poland. Remember, it was one of the Polish cloned Enigmas that eventually came to Bletchley Park. Prior to that, all Dilly Knox had to work on was an old commercial Enigma that was available on the open market with nowhere near the 159 quintillion (*long scale*) key possibilities.

Therefore to answer the question, it was the Polish code-breakers that broke the Enigma Code. Had they not done what they did, Bletchley Park may never have had the Enigma when it was most needed. We would have had to wait until we recovered a machine from somewhere. It would have been a vicious circle as we would have needed the intelligence from Enigma to find an Enigma. That undoubtedly would have extended the War and who knows that the outcome may have been?

Black Propaganda Radio

Dr Spieker was a German civil servant. During the 1930s, he was in the thick of the rise of the National Socialist movement (Nazi party). When Hitler rose to power on 30 January 1933, Dr Spieker, like many ordinary people in Germany, could see through Hitler's rhetoric. Many went along with it for a quiet life, and some rebelled, to their detriment. Whilst some got out before the proverbial mud hit the fan, Dr Spieker wanted to stand his ground and bring it home to the masses that they were being hoodwinked, and what Hitler and his Nazis were really about. Dr Spieker knew that he had no chance of setting up any kind of resistance from inside Germany, so he moved to France and joined one of the many freedom organisations that had grown there in response to the rise of fascism in Germany.

The organisation Dr Spieker became a part of set up a short-wave radio station to broadcast anti-Nazi propaganda into Germany. It was called *"Deutsche Freiheitssender" (German Freedom Station)*, and Dr Spieker became its main presenter. In May 1940, after the fall of France, it was becoming dangerous to operate this station with the Nazis approaching. With the assistance of French intelligence services, Dr Spieker spent a short time in the USA, and with the help of British Secret Intelligence Service (MI6) he was brought to Britain. He was given a new identity as Mr Turner and was asked to set up a propaganda radio station. These radio stations had the code-name of research units, or RUs. Mr Turner found himself sent to Whaddon Hall in Buckinghamshire.

Whaddon Hall was the top-secret radio station set up to transmit "Ultra", the deciphered enemy signals being disseminated and sent to our commanders in the theatre of war from the Government Code and Cipher School at Bletchley Park, just four and a half miles to the east. Whaddon Hall was shrouded in secrecy and run by MI6 section VIII communications. The head of section was Brigadier Richard Gambier-Parry, along with his chief engineer Harold K Robbin. This is where Mr Turner alias Dr Spieker setup his anti-Nazi radio station. The General Post Office laid a dedicated private wire to the transmitter station at Gawcott near Buckingham, approximately nine-and-a-half miles away. The Gawcott station had two 7.5 kW radio transmitters installed and would broadcast on the short-wave band directly into Germany.

In Germany, propaganda was an efficient and slickly-run organisation headed by Paul Joseph Goebbels, who controlled the complete media output of Nazi Germany including the newspapers, Cinema and broadcast radio. During the early part of the war, propaganda in Britain was a complete shambles. Many government departments all were overlapping, with many chiefs all trying to build up their own personal empires. In an attempt to bring all propaganda under one roof, a department was set up at a building in Victoria embankment in London: Electra House.

Electra House was owned by the General Post Office, and it was where the under-sea telegraph cables terminated from across the world. Cables were brought into London via the cable station in Porthcurno in Cornwall. At Electra House there was a vacant room number 207, and this was to become the headquarters of British propaganda. With the war lurking in the background, there was the worry of the London premises being bombed. So just like many other government departments, a suitable place in the country was searched for. The team at Electra house needed an official cover name so it was decided to simply call it department EH. One of the team was Leo Russell, a close relative of the Duke of Bedford, whose ancestral home was and still is Woburn Abbey in Bedfordshire. So with the right contacts, arrangements were made to move to Woburn Abbey, this became known as the Country Headquarters, or CHQ, and the main body of staff were told to meet at the Sugarloaf Hotel in Dunstable high-street where transport would be available to take them to CHQ, since the staff may have struggled to locate Woburn Abbey. This was because of wartime precautions that removed all signposts, so that if the Germans were to invade Britain, they would never find their way around and simply become lost!

Department EH at CHQ settled in to the converted riding stables. There were also offices in a house which was built for the Paris Trade Fair, and had been re-erected in the grounds of Woburn Abbey (today, this is a restaurant called "Paris house"). There were now at least three government departments dealing with propaganda: Department EH; Department MI (R), a government think tank; and section "D" (for destruction), a department in its early stages set up to perform sabotage, subversion, and general mayhem to the enemy. Things changed when Winston Churchill asked Alfred "Duff" Cooper, Minister of economic warfare, to set up one organisation to be in control of all subversion, sabotage, support of resistance groups, and propaganda. Churchill and Cooper did not see eye-to-eye at all. Many a row ensued then Churchill demanded to Cooper "just go and set Europe ablaze!"

Duff Cooper put together a team which became known as the Special Operations Executive, "SOE", and this replaced section "D". One Department of SOE was a propaganda section now known as S01, but there was already an organisation dealing with propaganda known as Department EH at Woburn Abbey. So it was decided to merge the two organisations into one efficient unit. This caused another debate, i.e. what to call the new propaganda division. Meetings were held, and arguments ensued. One of the members of the committee was David Bowes Lyon who just happened to be brother-in-law to King George VI. Bowes Lyon, having some persuasion, suggested to call the new organisation "the Political Warfare Executive". It was agreed and was officially formed on 9th October 1941.

There are different types and levels of propaganda:

Radio propaganda.

William Joyce was a member of the British Union of Fascists, who went to Germany to hobnob with the Nazis. He was set up with a propaganda radio station broadcasting his German rhetoric to Britain. His nickname was Lord Haw Haw, and his call-sign was *"Germany calling, Germany calling"*. His broadcast would contain anything from half-truths to outright lies. He would claim that certain British ships were being sunk and towns were being bombed. Joyce would ask on air "Why does Britain not just give up now and come round to the German way of life?" etc etc.

He would announce the same ships were being sunk, week after week! Nobody really believed him, he was more of a nuisance than of any great threat, but he got under people's skin enough to annoy them. However, justice caught up with him and he got his just deserts. On 28 May 1945 Joyce was captured by British forces at Flensburg, near the German border with Denmark. Spotting a disheveled figure while resting from gathering firewood, intelligence soldiers – including a Jewish German, Geoffrey Perry (born Horst Pinschewer), who had left Germany before the war – engaged him in conversation in French and English. After they asked whether he was Joyce, he reached for his pocket (actually reaching for a false passport); believing he was armed, they shot him through the buttocks, leaving four wounds. Two intelligence officers then drove him to a border post, and handed him to British military police. Joyce was then taken to London and tried at the Old Bailey on three counts of high treason and then executed.

Lord Haw Haw was just one example though, there was also "Axis Sally". She would do much the same things, but to the American troops during operation Torch in North Africa. Also, "Tokyo Rose", who broadcasted to the Americans in the Pacific.

Printed propaganda.

Another form of propaganda being used was of course the printed word. The German-language newspaper Nachrichten fur Truppe (Newspaper for German troops), was printed in England by the Home Counties Newspapers, in Luton Bedfordshire. This enabled us to give the German troops the news we wanted them to have. These papers were packed into bomb type containers known as Munro bombs, and dropped by the RAF over Germany from a safe height. The bombs had an altitude detonator which would blow the canister apart at the right point to distribute the newspapers over a very wide target area.

Forgery & Spreading rumors

This was another effective form of propaganda but more in the area of subversion. Prior to the war, Master forger Ellic Paul Howe collected many sets of Gothic typeface. During the war he was able to copy and produce any German document to an extremely high quality. Specific machinery was built to use the metric system to attain the correct paper size and print spacing. Special German watermark papers were smuggled into Britain which made it possible to print money and postage stamps, which showed a prominent head of someone other than Hitler. The stamps were very cleverly infiltrated into the German postal system. The public there did not realise that they were very illegal and were putting themselves in great danger by using them. Also food and clothing coupons were created, so that when these were filtered into the populace, they caused panic and confusion, since Germany had no rationing at that time.

Levels of propaganda.

Propaganda levels are identified with the colours White, Grey and Black. White propaganda is easily identifiable. It's clear where the message is coming from, and who is sending it, and the content is relatively unambiguous. An example would be the BBC World Service: although the BBC always purported to tell the truth it was always tilted to what we wanted the Germans to know. You could also say Lord Haw's radio station was white propaganda because we knew where it was coming from, even though we didn't think a lot of it, and certainly didn't believe it! Grey propaganda would not give you the location where it was coming from or which organisation was sending it. This was the case with Dr Spieker's *"Deutsche Freiheitssender"* the Germans had no idea where it was originating from, you cannot use direction-finding on shortwave transmissions unless you are very close by. With regards to Black propaganda, you make your recipient (the enemy) believe that the information is loyal to their cause, and that your messages are coming from somewhere within domain. In other words, a deception or a hoax, and our story is about Black propaganda radio.

Dennis Sefton Delmer plays the next part of this story.

Delmer known familiarly as "Tom", was born 1904 in Berlin, Germany, but was registered as a British citizen with the British Consulate. His parents were from Australia. His father, Frederick Sefton Delmer, born in Hobart, Tasmania, was Professor of English literature at Berlin University and author of a standard textbook for German schools. On the outbreak of the First World War his father was interned in Ruhleben internment camp as an enemy alien. In 1917, in a prisoner exchange between the British and German governments, the Delmer family was repatriated to England. Delmer, to this point, was educated at *Friedrichwerdersches Gymnasium*, Berlin, He began at St Paul's School London, and from there he won a scholarship to Lincoln College Oxford. After graduating with a second-class degree in modern languages, Delmer became a correspondent for the Daily Express newspaper in 1928, at the age of twenty-six. He was based at their Berlin bureau, and he spent most of his time in Berlin, where in the early 1930s, things were happening. When it was looking like the National Socialists were going to take power, Delmer travelled with Hitler and his cronies whilst canvassing and holding political meetings. He took some photographs of Hitler on his campaign trail; you know the thing, big smile, shake hands and kiss the baby, just like you've seen every politician do nowadays (*that's a warning from history*). Delmer could see through all this, he knew what Hitler was up to. When Delmer returned to England he tried to join MI6, the Secret Intelligence Service, as an agent based in Germany but was turned down owing to his close connections with Germany and its leaders. MI6 were concerned that he may be a Nazi sympathiser and possibly being paid and controlled by the German side.

Delmer continued to work for the Daily Express during the start of the war, and in early 1941, he was approached by Duff Cooper, the Minister for information. Cooper asked whether he would be interested to work for the BBC on a part-time basis on a Friday afternoon. It was a slot in the BBC World Service. The BBC was not in the business of delivering propaganda as such but it wanted Delmer to broadcast to Germany, in what we classed as white propaganda, since the Germans would know exactly where it was coming from and who was delivering it.

The BBC remained true to the slogan "Nation should speak peace unto nation", but programmes were still to be doctored to give our side of the story, and it was certainly sending coded messages to our agents via their special announcements. Delmer took the job, and his first broadcast was to be on Friday, 19th July 1940. His programme was to go out in the afternoon. Just a few hours earlier Adolf Hitler made a speech known as the "Coming to reason" speech, in which he said "I can see no reason why this war must go on. England (meaning Britain) should come round to our way of thinking!"

He seemed to not want to harm England, but instead to be comrades, and that we should trust him. On this summer's afternoon, Delmer sat in the studio at Bush house in London about to broadcast direct to Germany. All the Government ministers had gone to their country homes for the weekend there was no one at the ministries in Whitehall. Delmer decided via his first radio broadcast to send a reply himself to Adolf Hitler.

"Herr Führer, you have on occasion in the past consulted me as to the mood of the British public. So permit me to render

your Excellency this little service once again tonight. Let me tell you what we here in Britain think of this appeal of yours to what you are pleased to call our reason and common sense. *Herr Führer* and *Reichskanzler*, we throw it right back at you, right in to your evil smelling teeth
(*Black Boomerang Sefton Delmer. An Autobiography volume 2*)

Well, that really caused the mud to hit the Whitehall ministry fans, Ministers were recalled over the weekend. Questions were asked in the house, "Who is this Delmer anyway?" Many senior figures in Parliament were listening to Hitler and possibly believing some of his rhetoric.

...Duff Cooper rallied to my support with all his suave authority. He assured the House that my talk had the Cabinet's full approval. And when the Foreign Secretary Lord Halifax replied to Hitler a couple of days after me the sense of what he said was the same, although he used rather more restrained language.
(*Black Boomerang*)

Later in the week Lord Halifax, the Foreign Secretary, stood up in Parliament and virtually repeated Delmer's words. After that the whole incident was brushed under the carpet. The Gestapo kept a list of all the people they would arrest should they ever invade Britain, known as the wanted list or *Sonderfahndungsliste GB*. Sefton Delmer's name was added to this list. But Delmer believed that his name was on the list anyway.

After that, MI6 wanted to give Delmer his chance to become an agent. They asked him to go to the Portuguese capital, Lisbon, and pose as a Daily Express reporter.

"I *am* a Daily Express reporter," he replied.

The job was actually to report on refugees leaving Germany by escaping through Lisbon, which was neutral in the war. In particular, anyone who worked for the electronic companies Ascania and Lorenz in Germany. He had barely started his newly-found occupation as an agent (spy), when he received a telegram from Leonard Ingrams, the under-secretary at the Ministry of economic warfare. Delmer was asked to return to England as soon as possible where an important job awaited him. Delmer returned to Britain and was sent to the country headquarters CHQ of the Political Warfare Executive at Woburn Abbey. Delmer was asked to sign the official secrets act, and it has been reported that while he was in the office there was a telephone call for Delmer from Lord Beaverbrook, the owner of the Daily Express newspapers. Beaverbrook had been informed where Delmer was, and quizzed him about the appointment. "How much money are they paying you there?" Beaverbrook enquired.

Delmer said, "I can't tell you as I have just signed the official secrets act." Beaverbrook was absolutely furious that anyone would refuse one of his requests, and a row ensued over the telephone. Beaverbrook was so annoyed over this episode he didn't speak to Delmer at all through the rest of the war. After the PWE had finished with Delmer at Woburn, he was chauffeur-driven back to London in a Rolls-Royce, and he was told that he could keep the car until his next job was organised and ready for him. He was of course curious, but they advised him, "As you know everything is top secret here, or hush-hush, as we say." And they wouldn't enlighten him further. "Go to London. You will be on full pay, we have an office for you, just off Berkeley Square." Delmer had to hang about for two months before he was told anything.

Delmer's First RU

Delmer was finally asked to make his way to Wavendon Towers, near the village of Simpson in North Buckinghamshire, 5 miles north-west of Woburn Abbey. Wavendon Towers was to eventually house the headquarters of the Milton Keynes development Corporation, but back in 1941 it was a large country house.

In the converted billiard room, Delmer was asked to set up his own R.U. (research unit or propaganda radio station). With his history of being outspoken, and his German fluency, he was given carte blanche. Delmer took complete advantage of that. The first thing he noticed that there were many RUs operating from Britain already. They were extremely amateur and seemed to be not very effective. Delmer maintained that they were broadcasting to the wrong people: there is no way that you are going to have any impact or influence whatsoever over the minds of committed members of the SS, Gestapo, or any other senior Nazis. However by pretending to support Germany, and Hitler as its leader, whilst denouncing the culture of the Nazis as corrupt, Delmer's station gained

103

interest, and people started to listen. He broadcast about Nazis hoarding cash, hiding private bank accounts in Switzerland, obtaining food and clothing coupons for personal use, and also accused them of peddling pornography and narcotics, sometimes using extreme and explicit language, which was compelling and shocking.

Those German people who were most likely to become anti-Nazi were not those who were benefiting from their terrible regime of hate, fear, violence and death, but those who were affected by it, these would be Delmer's target audience. His scriptwriters were to be German refugees who had escaped just in time to come to Britain. Many were journalists, writers, novelists. One such person was Peter Seckelmann, who was to become the radio station's main presenter. Local houses were acquisitioned to house all the staff; script writers, the engineers and the presenters, in the nearby villages of Aspley Guise and Woburn Sands, which were also close to CHQ Woburn Abbey Bedfordshire.

Prisoners-of-war are also useful for information. Put them in a room together and they will talk. British intelligence would bug their rooms and record their conversations. Information was obtained from prisoner-of-war units based at Latimer House in Amersham, Wooten Park in Beaconsfield (both in Buckinghamshire), and also Trent Park in Cockfosters (then Middlesex now Hertfordshire). Some of the information was passed to Delmer. The official name of Delmer's new station was RU/G3 but Delmer gave the station its own call sign GS1 *Gustav Siegfried Eines*. It didn't mean anything at all; Delmer had just made it up as it made it sound like an official radio station. The programs were recorded at the studios at Wavendon Towers. As the studio was close to the village of Simpson, the studio GS1 would be known as the "Simpsons".

The programs were recorded onto RCA 18-inch glass discs. Each disc could record a maximum of twenty minutes, so this limitation decided the length of the program. The glass discs worked in the opposite way to a normal gramophone record. You would put the stylus in the centre and it would run to the outer side. When the needle reached the edge of the record it would drop off onto a buffered pad. The reason for this was that the recording was supposed to sound like a live broadcast. With a normal gramophone record you would hear the shushing sound as the needle reached the end of the record. Once the recordings were made they would be sent to the transmitting station by dispatch rider. These riders were specially screened and selected since this was a high-security operation.

A new transmission station was set up at the village of Potsgrove just a few miles south of Simpson. Here there were two more 7.5kW transmitters installed and to backup the station at Gawcott near Buckingham. On 23rd May 1941, the station was ready to roll. Peter Seckelmann was given the *nom-de-plume* Paul Saunders, and Delmer gave Paul Saunders the On-Air name of "Der Chef". This was the name that Hitler was referred to as by his lackeys behind his back. Delmer knew this from Hitler's campaigning days. This was a professional radio station with a signature tune, and after the music faded away, Paul Saunders would announce "this is *Gustav Siegfried Eines*.... this is *Gustav Siegfried Eins*....." then proceed with the program.

Just twelve days before the station went on the air, Adolf Hitler's deputy Rudolf Hess flew into Scotland on a peace mission on 11th May 1941. This was apparently his own doing and without the authority of Adolf Hitler. Der Chef's first big broadcast was to announce a welcome to Rudolf Hess in Scotland. At the same time he told his audience all the names of the people responsible in Germany for arranging Rudolf Hess's operation. The story was fabricated but the names were genuine. Because of the information received from our intelligence services, it was revealed that the Gestapo rounded up all the names on Delmer's list. They were then arrested for interrogation. This was good news for GS1 as they then knew that the Germans were listening in. Der Chef always made his listeners believe that GS1 radio stations were being chased by the Gestapo, even though they made their listeners believe the station was coming from inside Germany. It was obvious to the German radio monitors that the station was probably being broadcast from Britain. Even the American embassy reported back to Washington of the existence of an anti-Nazi radio station transmitting in Germany called *Gustav Siegfried Eines.*

The German authorities were becoming concerned about GS1 and all of the other propaganda stations being set up in many different parts of Europe. They instituted a ban on anyone listening to any radio stations coming from outside Germany. In other words you were not allowed to listen to programs on the shortwave bands (Long Distance Transmissions). However programs within Germany were broadcast on the medium wave band. Such as the Fuehrer's "people radio station". It was made illegal for anybody to listen to foreign radio stations. A new radio receiver was introduced and distributed by the German authorities which had only the medium-wave band, so you could only listen to programs from within Germany. On the front of the radio was an orange label which stated that it is a crime to listen to foreign radio stations, punishable by hard labour. Later, the punishment was death. However if you were a senior member of the Nazi party you could purchase a small adapter that would plug-in to a socket at the rear of your people's radio set, and could enable such an authorised person to tune into any radio station they wished.

GS1 continued to broadcast and be a thorn in the side of the Nazis, and the station used extremely bad language that had never been heard on any radio station before. Depending on conditions, some of these GS1 transmissions could also be picked up in Britain. It was soon becoming clear that the programs contained some extreme and shocking content, describing obscene situations that it was said the Nazis were involved with, backed up with filthy language. It wasn't long before this was being reported to the British authorities, and the government became aware. Stafford Cripps, a member of the British Cabinet and privy Seal, wrote to Anthony Eden, an executive member of the PWE to complain that "if this sort of thing is required to win the war, I would rather lose it". But Delmer's program, was strongly supported by Robert Bruce Lockhart, director of the Political Warfare Executive. Delmer made it clear that nothing in the Geneva Convention was being contravened, and also that this part of his broadcasts would attract the younger soldiers to listen in, and be taken in with a more subtle propaganda messages that were being sent.

The German propaganda ministry was run by Joseph Goebbels, and they put out a series of leaflets warning German people not to listen to illegal radio stations, because "Rumours come out of the airwaves like complainers come out of the woodwork". Our forgery department copied the leaflet to the absolute word, font and style, but added the words "only listen to official stations like *Gustav Siegfried Eines*". Then the RAF dropped the leaflets over towns and cities in Germany. By this point, Der Chef was up to new tricks, reading out personal messages as if they were sent in to the radio station. But once again this was all fabricated, just like the listeners' letters and replies that he gave. One such message read that there was to be a meeting at the Union Cinema on a particular night. There were many Union Cinemas across Germany, and of course he didn't state which one would be hosting this imaginary meeting. The idea was to give the Gestapo something to worry about, and they sent their black leather coated officers on a wild goose chase to many Union Cinemas looking for a meeting that didn't exist. At least it kept them on their toes.

GS1 programs were twenty minutes in duration. This was dictated by the recording time of the RCA discs. The engineers at the transmitting station would play the discs, and then repeated the programs later in the day. One of Delmer's distasteful outbursts on-air was to show his alliance to Hitler. He stated that "Winston Churchill was a flat-footed bastard of a drunken Jew" and King George VI "was a stuttering fool." After two-and-a-half years of broadcasting, it was time for GS1 to close down, as bigger things were on the horizon. Delmer always made it clear that the station was being chased by the Gestapo. So to end the station's life they staged an elaborate piece of theatre, a mock attack by the Gestapo to finish off *Gustav Siegfried Eines*. On 18th of November 1943, the listeners heard the studio door smashed down, the sound of someone shouting *Schweinehund*!! Followed by the sound of machine gun fire, *rat a tat tat tat!!!* The station then went dead. Which was all a good idea but no one thought to advise the radio engineers about the station closing down, as later in the day the engineers repeated the broadcast. I don't suppose we will ever know if anybody noticed.

Owing to the Draconian measures in Germany regarding listening to any radio station other than official People's radio station (the Nazi radio station) we needed another way to get our British propaganda into the homes of the ordinary German people. An idea was to try and broadcast on the same wavelengths as the German People's programme. Up until now, we were transmitting on shortwave, and the distance we had to cover was achieved easily using relatively low-powered 7.5 kW shortwave transmitters. The German Peoples Programme was transmitted on medium-wave transmitters from within Germany. To transmit locally on medium wavelengths can be done on relatively low power. If the Political Warfare Executive wanted to transmit from Britain to Germany on medium wave this would require an extremely high-powered transmitter. The development cost alone would make the building of one of these impossible. So the PWE took a look further afield.

The head of MI6 section VIII communications Brigadier Gambier Parry, was an ex-employee of the Philco electronics company, and he had contacts in the USA. Gambier Parry, who was also the head of technical control for the PWE, knew through his contacts that the RCA Company of America had built a 500 kW transmitter for a commercial radio station in the USA. But owing to recent US legislation, station, WJZ in New Jersey were not permitted to use a medium-wave transmitter of such high power. Gambier Parry, knowing what the PWE were looking for, sent his chief engineer Harold Robin to the RCA factory in the United States. Negotiations took place, a deal was done, the transmitter was to be upgraded to 600 kW and the PWE were authorised to pay the RCA Company of America £65,000. This was to become the most powerful medium-wave radio transmitter in Europe at the time. The transmitter was given the name Aspidistra, named after the Gracie Fields song the "Biggest Aspidistra in the world".

It must be emphasised that a radio transmitter is not simply the aerials you see above ground. Aspidistra would require a massive underground building to house the enormous cabinets that would contain the gigantic transmitting valves (US vacuum tubes). The enormous temperatures generated required special high-powered cooling system and the cabinets containing the valves would have to be lined with lead owing to the lethal x-rays which would be emitted from the tubes. To protect Aspidistra from air raids the plan was to build the transmitting station underground in a disused gravel quarry near the proposed studio at Milton Bryan, close to Woburn Abbey. It was felt that the Aspidistra should in fact be closer to the continent, so another site was eventually found at Kingstanding, close to Crowborough in Surrey. When the BBC got wind of this they were furious. They, along with the air Ministry complained to the General Post Office who licensed all radio transmitters in Britain. They stated that should the Germans discover what we were doing, transmitting on German frequencies at high power to jam the German broadcast radio, the Germans would retaliate and plan to jam the BBC! The Germans never had a transmitter of this power and were very unlikely to ever build one, owing to the costs and time required, since they were far too busy developing new weapons.

Eventually a deal was struck with the BBC. This would allow the BBC to use the transmitter during the day for external broadcast programmes. Then the PWE could use the station at other times. Aspidistra was not only very powerful, it was extremely versatile and could change frequencies in seconds.

Up until now, radio transmitters of this power never had this facility. To install Aspidistra at Kingstanding, a seventy acre site was found, and a fifty foot deep hole was evacuated. This was achieved by six-hundred Canadian Army engineers stationed close by. It took nine months of working around the clock to complete. The transmitter equipment was brought over from the United States by the Royal Navy, one consignment had to be reordered because one of the ships had been torpedoed and sunk. Eventually, the three-hundred foot masts were erected. There were also up to 100 kW mobile transmitters used at different locations to confuse the German direction-finding units. The studio complex which was still to be at Milton Bryan was completed by the Ministry of Works.

There were two different ideas for programmes: One was to entertain the German troops and U-Boat crews on leave and the second was to break through the German medium-wave radio frequencies and broadcast straight onto the People's radio channels. Two new radio stations were set up to transmit programmes, the first one was called "Atlantic sender", which would be aimed at the U-boat crews on leave. Second program would be called *"Soldaltensender Calais"* later to be called *"Soldaltensender West"* this would be aimed mainly at soldiers and infantrymen on leave, and broadcast into their *canteens.*

The programmes consisted of American jazz, which had been banned because of the involvement of Jewish and black musicians, but the music itself was well-liked and well listened to. There were also news items from Germany, which were genuine but subtly laced with propaganda. An example of this type of broadcast was a news item telling the German people "if you have your food coupons, queues are already mounting at shops, so please be early." The truth of the matter was that the food coupons were not even in use, and this caused panic. Other messages were to include reports of a particular city had been bombed. This of course was true. But the casualty figures in certain areas were falsely inflated. Items also included that typhoid was breaking out in bombed cities, also actual sports results and news of decorations awarded such as the Iron Cross, also true. Another false feature was to say that prisoners-of-war were earning very high wages in the USA. Genuine information was laced with propaganda, which was subtle, black propaganda at its best. There were just enough discrepancies in the news to lower morale, making the German people think "is this war really worth fighting?" This was all cleverly and carefully put across to try and create an impression of failure. The servicemen who heard this news would believe that their families were suffering even more than they were, and it made them demoralised. The programs were carefully designed to make the Germans believe the radio station was credible.

So how was Delmer obtaining all this genuine information? One way was German newspapers or even our agents sending information back to us. Before the war, almost all newspapers had their main presses in Fleet Street London, and the German press had their offices and journalists there. When war was announced, they fled back to Germany, leaving all their offices intact and even leaving a machine behind called the "*Hellschriber*". This was a type of radio teleprinter, operated with a radio signal received from the German news agency in Berlin, which was now controlled by Joseph Goebbels' propaganda ministry. The "*Hellschriber*" machine was sent up to Delmer's studio at Milton Bryan where he had the latest German news before it was even printed in the German newspapers. Aspidistra went live on 8th November 1942, the first programmes on *Atlanticsender* were transmitted on 22nd March 1943 and *Soldaltensender* went on air 24th October 1943, both stations were broadcast on the medium-wave band. They also shared the official name of RU/G9, which was transmitted on 360 meters, 420 meters and 490 meters. The main presenter was Vicky, real name Agnes Bernelle, a refugee who escaped Nazi Germany and the Holocaust.

Intrusion operations.

This was yet another plan to send black propaganda into the homes of everyday German families. In Germany it was a serious offence to listen to foreign shortwave radio stations, people were only allowed to listen to the medium wave bands with German programs. To help ensure this you could only purchase medium wave radios, as in the People's radio set. Although many people did take the risk, we needed to get into the homes and minds of as many people as possible. This was a period of time where we were bombing German cities. Hitler believed that the British bombers were using German broadcast radio transmitters as navigational beacons, since this information had been passed to the German authorities via the British Double Cross System (MI5 B1a). So the Germans shut down certain medium wave radio transmitters which they believed were being used in this way. This encouraged the German authorities to shut down transmitters in a particular city. The consequence would be that the population of that city found their local programs suddenly fading out. Other radio transmitters broadcasting the National programme in other parts of Germany would still be operating as normal.

The PWE would use very sensitive receiving aerials to pick up the German national station from German transmitters that were still operating using the medium waveband, then they would boost the signal, and then re-transmit it with very high power back to Germany using the Aspidistra transmitter. If you are now wondering, what was the point of re-transmitting German programmes' back into Germany, the reason is as follows. We sent their programmes. Back probably in better quality than some of their own radio stations. On the hour Milton Bryan would fade-out the German news program and we would then fade-in the news broadcasts that we wanted the Germans to hear. We were now broadcasting right into the homes of German families, on their own radio frequencies. The operation was very successful, and after the war we learned from German people that they were completely unaware that they had been listening to black propaganda radio. And of course we never admitted to them that fact, because it was a closely-guarded secret.

By May 1945 the PWE ordered the closing down of all RUs or research units (propaganda radio stations). There were no formal announcements, they just went off the air. At Milton Bryan, machinery was dismantled and disposed of, whilst paperwork and other documents, including scripts, were burnt within the grounds. Everything had to remain secret and classified for many years afterwards. The houses in Aspley Guise and Woburn Sands were returned for domestic use, and the Duke of Bedford brought his home back to how it was prior to the war. Eventually he opened it to the public to help pay for massive land taxes. Woburn Abbey now is a beautiful stately home and attracts many visitors. One of the buildings within the grounds of Woburn Abbey that had been occupied by the PWE, has now become an exclusive restaurant. The studios at Milton Bryan are now the headquarters of a local Scout Troop. Aspidistra, the largest medium-wave broadcast transmitter in Europe at that time, was now to be used by the BBC external services, then by the Diplomatic Wireless Service. Eventually, the transmitter was offered as a donation to the London Science Museum but turned down. Some parts went to the BBC transmitting station at Orfordness Suffolk, the rest was dismantled and scrapped, and the aerials were taken down. The underground site was converted to a cold war Bunker as one of the 17 locations in England and Wales to be used as seats of regional government in the event of a nuclear attack. Then used temporarily by the Sussex police, and eventually became an underground warehousing facility.

Denis Sefton Delmer, for a short time made up some of his differences with Lord Beaverbrook. He returned to Fleet Street as foreign affairs reporter for the Daily Express newspaper. Tom, as Delmer was known at the Express, edited virtually every foreign story during the 1950s for the Daily Express. After a row over expenses, Delmer was fired in 1959 by Lord Beaverbrook. He retired to Lamarsh in Essex. "THIS IS YOUR LIFE - Denis Sefton Delmer, journalist and foreign correspondent", said Eamonn Andrews outside the Caprice restaurant in London's Mayfair. Broadcast live: Mon 8 Jan 1962. He became an author and wrote many books, which included two volumes of his biography: "Trail Sinister" 1961 "Black Boomerang" 1962. Dennis Sefton Delmer died on 4th September 1979 at the age of 75.

Did Black Propaganda Radio work?

From reports attained after the war, the programs of *Gustav Siegfried Eines, Atlanticsender* and *Soldatonsender Calais,* were very popular and well listened to. But one thing is for sure, just like Operation Overlord was Britain's biggest deception, Black Propaganda Radio was Britain's biggest hoax.

Sink the Bismarck!

Germany made a strategic error in 1934. Prior to the Second World War, in a serious flaw of judgment, Adolf Hitler agreed to build two of the largest, costly and the most technically advanced battleships in the world at that time. It was to break the conditions of the 1919 Treaty of Versailles, which Hitler claimed to be a stab in the back for Germany. The Treaty allowed Germany just enough military strength to defend its territory, with conditions of no U-boats, no air-force, the limit of one hundred thousand troops, including the maximum size of any capital warships, not to be in excess of 40,000 tons. Then further reductions to 35,000 tons after the Washington and London Naval treaties. By Hitler publicly denouncing the treaty, alarm bells should have been ringing in Whitehall. Germany was building up its military at a breakneck speed. Britain watched and waited.

The two battleships would well exceed the treaty's stated maximum size. They were to be named the Bismarck – after the 19th Century "Iron Chancellor" Otto von Bismarck who unified Germany from many *Prussian* states. The other battleship would be called *Tirpitz* after Germany's first nineteenth century Grand Admiral, Alfred von Tirpitz. Hitler's plan was that if the situation resulted in a war with Britain, Germany would use these mighty battleships along with U-boats to destroy Britain's merchant fleets. These fleets were bringing vital supplies from the Americas, the Empire and from around the world via sea trading routes that had been established for hundreds of years. Though both battleships were intended to be ready at the same time for maximum impact, *Kriegsmarinewerft Wilhelmshaven* where *Tirpitz* was being built was running a month late. The *Bismarck* however was launched on 14th February 1939 and commissioned into the *Kriegsmarine* August 1940. The story of the *Bismarck* was told in a very good Twentieth Century Fox film of 1960 starring Kenneth Moore and Dana Wynter, "Sink the Bismarck!" But the story told was only a synopsis as the full operation involved 64 ships, including 32 of the home fleet. Six of the Western approaches command, five Plymouth command, one from Nor command, nine from Force H, two from America and Indies Station. One from South Atlantic Command and 8 from the submarine service. The part in the Film played by Kenneth Moore was actually commanded by Captain Ralph Edwards (later Admiral Sir Ralph Edwards KCB, CBE).

Background

Let's take a step back for a moment to the early days of the Royal Navy. From Tudor times (the Navy Royal) consisted of great wooden battleships built of solid oak, armed with iron cannons, of which the ammunition consisted of heavy iron balls. The cannonballs would be fired out of the cannons with a charge of gunpowder, a dull grey powder which was extremely volatile when ignited in a confined space. The power of the cannons could punch a hole through the thick oak of your enemy's ships. This type of ammunition was used in slightly modified forms right up to the manufacture of steel-hulled ships in the mid nineteenth century, where Gunpowder had been replaced by cordite, a more powerful and less smoky explosive. Then the designs of ammunition changed to an aerodynamic shape which could pierce through the steel hull of a modern warship. This weapon, known as a shell, was filled with high-explosives which once entering the enemy vessel would explode, the splinters of which would cause untold damage to life, machinery and also igniting stored weapons. This type of ammunition was used very successfully in the First World War, especially in May 1916 in the Battle of Jutland.

Traditional methods of battle formation would be for ships to turn broadside on, to give the minimum deck target from ether direct hits or plunging shells. If a shell penetrates the deck, this could cause a serious fire, possibly igniting the ship's magazine. In 1939, the Royal Navy was without doubt the largest Navy in the world. Germany's Navy was modern, small, and with very little experience. So why did Adolf Hitler think in his wildest dreams that the Royal Navy would allow these two new battleships to survive?

KMS Bismarck

With kind permission The Imperial War Museum

KMS Bismarck

The *Bismarck*'s armament consisted of four main gun turrets each containing 2 x 380mm (15") cannons, each weighing 1,900 tons, 2 on the stern named Anton & Bruno, two on the aft Caesar & Dora, with a further forty-four side cannons, including anti-aircraft guns. On board were four Arado 196 float airoplanes used for recognisance. These planes could be launched from catapult ramps at the side of the ship. The planes returned to the ship when they would then be brought back on board by one of the two side cranes. *Bismarck* had an armored deck that was 120mm thick, also armored steel belt of 320mm thick was wrapped around the ship to protect the ship from torpedo attack. *Bismarck* was 251m in length, with a beam of 36m. Three turbine engines could produce 150,000 horse-power, with a fuel capacity of 8000 tons. This gave *Bismarck* a range at 16 knots (18.4mph) of 9000 miles (approximately 1.1 ton of fuel per mile). She weighed 45,000 tons, 55,000 tons fully laden. *Bismarck*'s main turrets could fire a shell weighing almost one ton, the distance of nineteen miles, which is over the horizon. *Bismarck* was also equipped with basic forward-facing radar and an advanced gunnery computing system.

On 16th November 1935 the building contract was placed with the Blohm & Voss Shipyard in Hamburg, construction number BV 509, then 1st July 1936 the keel was laid on slipway 9 at Blohm & Voss. *Bismarck* was launched thirty-one months later on 14th February 1939, Valentine's Day, by Dorothea von Lowenfeld the granddaughter of Otto von *Bismarck*. Followed by grand celebrations to which Hitler, Himler along with the rest of the Nazi hierarchy were present, especially Joseph Goebbels head of the Nazi propaganda Ministry to publicise this major event. As the ship slid down into the river Elbe the *Bismarck* went for fitting out. *Bismarck* was commissioned into the *Kriegsmarine* August 1940. Her only commander was to be Otto Ernst Lindemann, who joined the German Imperial Navy in 1913 as a telegraph officer and worked his way up through the ranks to become captain of Germany's greatest battleship. In September 1940 *Bismarck* was put through her sea trials in the Baltic, then returning to Hamburg in December 1940 to complete her final fitting. The final fitting-out consisted of bunk-beds, lavatories, galleys, shoe-menders, dental and medical areas including a full operating theatre. Also, tailor's shop, a cinema, radio station, not forgetting the ship's newspaper press (*"Die Schiffglocke"* The Ship's Bell). This was a cruise-ship battleship, the pride of the German navy, the best that money could buy. You could say that this was the battleship that Harrods would sell you. With all that came the bill for 71,642,000 Deutschmarks, a real bargain!

Rheinunbung

1st March 1941, *Bismarck* transits the Kiel Canal for the last time from Hamburg to Gothenhafen (Polish Gadynia) to complete her final sea trials. On 5th May 1941, Adolf Hitler inspects the crew. Spending as little time as possible on the ship as ships whether at sea or in a harbour made him sea sick. 12th May 1941. Admiral Gunter Lutjens raises his flag on *Bismarck* to prepare for what was to become *Bismarck*'s one and only operation, Exercise Rhine (*"Rheinunbung"*). The plan was to sail from Germany to the North Atlantic, without detection and to avoid conflict with the Royal Navy at all costs, unless of course if under attack. Once in the Atlantic, her orders were to destroy as much British merchant shipping as possible. With two massive battleships probably to be backed up with U-boats and heavy cruisers in the Atlantic we could have had major problems. The aim of this operation was to starve Britain into surrender. Britain, unlike Germany, is an island nation and was only one third self-sufficient, therefore surviving on food and minerals from across the globe. Britain's trading routes were now under the most serious threat of annihilation. The original idea was for the *Bismarck* and her sister ship the *Tirpitz* to be ready at the same time. Manufacturing delays caused *Tirpitz* to be two months behind schedule. The *Kriegsmarine* made the decision to continue with exercise Rhine without *Tirpitz*, but instead, *Bismarck* was to be paired with the heavy cruiser "*Prinz Eugen*".

Day 1

Sunday 18th May 1941 was the first day of Exercise Rhine, *Bismarck* left Gothenhafen at 12 noon. At the commencement of *Rheinunbung*. Some of the crew's families stood on the quayside on the cold, overcast spring day, probably never suspecting they were waving their loved ones goodbye for the last time.

Day 2

Monday 19th May 1941. *Bismarck* is at sea and joined by *Prinz Eugen*. At 2330 three destroyers accompanied the naval task force. Before *Bismarck* left Gothenhafen, there was an accident while taking on fuel, a pipe burst losing 200 tons of fuel. A decision was taken not to fix the problem, but to refuel from a supply ship "*Wollin*" waiting at Grimstafjord near Bergen, so *Bismarck* started this operation without her full fuel capacity.

Day 3

Tuesday 20th May 1941. As the task force headed into Kattegat and north along the Great Dutch Belt, she was accompanied by the *Luftwaffe* for further protection. The British radio monitoring stations "Y" stations were receiving a high proportion of radio traffic coming from the Baltic region. This was immediately passed to Bletchley Park for code-breaking and traffic analysis. Traffic analysis was passed down to the Operations Intelligence Centre (OIC) at the Citadel the underground planning and control room beneath the Admiralty Building in London. It appeared from intelligence reports that German capital warships were in transit and heading for the North Sea. More reports were arriving at the OIC, this time from Captain Henry Denham, the British Naval attaché in Stockholm. Stating that the Swedish ship *Gotland* had also spotted the flotilla, then a message was received from a Norwegian resistance worker

Viggo Alexon also locating the ships. At the OIC, Captain Ralph Edwards was given the task of controlling this operation. He decided that virtually without doubt, this group of ships was led by the new German battleship *Bismarck*.

Day 4

Wednesday 21st May 1941 The *Seekampfgruppe* lead by *Bismarck* enters Korsfjord an arm of Grimstadfjord then moors up, this is close to Bergen. The crew paint the ship into its Atlantic camouflage, known as battleship Grey. At 1315 an RAF coastal command reconnaissance Spitfire aircraft flies at 26,000ft and takes amazing photographs of *Bismarck* and other ships at rest in the fjord. Admiral Lutjens once again turned down an opportunity to refuel from the supply ship *Wollin*. Lutjens felt that Hitler had gotten wind of *Bismarck* leaving without *Tirpitz* and may have been thinking of recalling *Bismarck* and possibly postponing operation. Lutjen's wanted to get cracking, as he knew that there were numerous German fuel-supply ships waiting in the North Atlantic. So he decided to press on.

The pictures taken of *Bismarck* by flying officer Michael Suckling were hastily sent to the Admiralty. But Lutjens was on the move.

Day 5

Thursday 22nd May 1941. *Bismarck* was sailing North at 24knots. Admiral Lutjens addresses the crew over the tannoy system, he advises the young, fairly inexperienced seamen of *Bismarck*'s "Operation Rhine", that they would be raiding merchant ships that were supplying Britain with food, oil, armaments.

Lutjens now had the choice of four routes to access the Atlantic from the Norwegian Sea;

1. Between the Orkney Islands and the Shetlands. But that would be too close to the Royal naval base at Scappa Flow

2. Between the Shetland Isles and the Faroe Islands

3. The Faroe's Gap between Iceland and the Faroe Islands. This, in theory, should have been his best choice, but he chose this fourth route:

4. The Denmark Straits, between Greenland and Iceland.

This was a more treacherous route as it was laden with icebergs, even though most of the ice had broken up by this time of the year, Lutjens knew this route as he took the *Sharnhorst* and *Gneisenhau* battle cruisers this way earlier in the year for Operation Berlin (January 1941). Which was a similar and successful sortie in the Atlantic, where they sank 22 merchant ships totaling of 115,000 tons.

In the meantime, the RAF had been ordered to bomb *Bismarck* which they believed was still moored at Grimstadfjord. When the bombers arrived, there was heavy cloud, so they attempted some carpet bombing through the clouds, hoping they might make a lucky hit on target. However, as the cloud cleared, it was obvious that the German fleet had gone. The Commander-in-Chief of the home fleet Admiral Jack Tovey received the news and put a task force in place. The Germans, suspecting that they may have been spotted, decided to take some reconnaissance pictures of Scappa Flow. The Germans knew if there were many Royal naval Capital ships in the Scappa it would be conceivable that they may not have been spotted. If that was the case Exercise Rhine would be safe. The recognisance photographs were taken by the *Luftwaffe* which showed many capital ships were still in port. But what they failed to realise was that they had been caught out by the oldest trick in the Royal Navy's book, the capital ships they photographed from 20,000 feet were mainly wood and canvas decoys.

Tovey puts to sea

Tovey's flagship was the newly-built battleship *HMS King George V* She would sail with the aircraft carrier *HMS Victorious,* Admiral Sir Lancelot Holland, would sail with *HMS Hood* and *HMS Prince of Wales.* Also on constant patrol in the Denmark Straits were the cruisers *HMS Norfolk* and *HMS Suffolk,* controlled by Admiral Wake-Walker. *HMS Suffolk* was fitted with the latest advance Radar which could scan 270° unlike the *Bismarck*'s fixed forward Radar. *HMS Renown* was called in from the Clyde. *HMS Hood* and *HMS Prince of Wales* were heading for the south of Iceland, with *"KG5"* and *Victorious* following on. Meanwhile, *Suffolk* and *Norfolk* patrolling the Denmark Straits kept receiving false alarms due to their radar and visual reports wrongly identifying icebergs as ships on the horizon.

There were many other Royal Naval ships in this operation they are all listed at the end of this chapter.

Day 6.

Friday 23rd May 1941. *Norfolk* and *Suffolk* are patrolling the Denmark Straights in and out of thick banks of sea fog caused by the melting ice and the warmer air temperature. At 19.22 able seaman Newall spots *Bismarck* and "Action Stations" are sounded. The cruisers would be no match for *Bismarck*, so a safe distance was kept. At 20.30, *Bismarck* spotted the cruisers and opened fire. This was the first time the *Bismarck* had fired her guns in anger, and all shots missed their target. The cruisers reduced their speed and kept to a safe distance, using their Radar to assist tracking. Signals were sent back to the Admiralty and passed on to Tovey. The firing had caused a technical issue on *Bismarck* as the intense vibration from firing her cannons seriously damaged her Radar equipment, which the on-board engineers could not repair. *Bismarck*'s escort *ship Prinz Eugen* had radar, so it was decided by Lutjens that as he could not sail radar blind *Prinz Eugen* should over-take *Bismarck* and lead the operation. As *Prinz Eugen* sailed past *Bismarck, Bismarck's* state of the art electric steering wheel failed. There was a near miss as these two mighty German warships almost collided. Had that happened our story would of ended here. It should be mentioned that the two German ships looked a very similar shape from a distance, even though they were vastly different in size.

Day 7 Battle of Denmark Straits.

Saturday 24th May 1941. *HMS Hood* & *HMS Prince of Wales* were now approximately 225 miles west of Iceland, on course to intercept *Bismarck* & *Prinz Eugen*. *HMS Hood* was built in Glasgow in 1917 and was completely overhauled in 1920. This powerful battleship was not a battleship but a battle-cruiser. She lacked enough armour had very little side protection and virtually no deck armour. This would have made her easy prey to a plunging shell, but she had 8 massive 15" cannons. She was slightly longer but slightly slower than *Bismarck*. She had mainly been used to promote Britain around the empire, "Look at our navy, we are big and powerful! Woe betide anyone who starts trouble with Britain!" As *HMS Hood* travelled the British Empire parties and guided tours were held on-board. People were proud that such a powerful ship could protect them that is why she became known as the "Pride of the Royal Navy" The *Prince of Wales* was a new battleship, but not without big problems, her main turrets were not functioning correctly. When she left Scappa Flow, civilian engineers from Vickers Armstrong were still onboard; they were going to be on a cruise of a lifetime.

At 0552 *Hood* and *Prince of Wales* spot and open fire on what they thought was *Bismarck*, but if you recall, the *Prinz Eugen* was now the leading ship and their outlines were very similar. 0554 *Prinz Eugen* opens fire on *Hood*, all shells missed. 0555, *Bismarck* opens fire on the *Hood*. The first four salvos miss, but *Bismarck*'s fifth salvo caused a plunging hit which penetrated *Hood*'s aft deck and started a fire. This happened Just as *Hood* was repositioning to a broadside-on position to try to avoid this extremely dangerous situation from occurring. The fire spread very quickly to the ship's magazine via apparent open flame traps which were left open to hasten the bringing of the ammunition between the magazine and the big guns. A massive explosion occurred as a powerful jet of flames burst upwards. As the *Hood's* magazine had ignited the tremendous downward force of the explosion broke the ship in two. At 0601 just nine minutes into the battle HMS *Hood* had sunk without trace, with the loss of 1,421 officers and men. There were just three survivors; even the Germans were amazed at how quickly the pride of the Royal Navy went to the bottom. *Bismarck* now turned its guns onto the *Prince of Wales*, which as it happens the Germans wrongly identified as *KG5*. The Germans opened intense and accurate fire on *Prince of Wales*, with 15-inch, 8-inch and 5.9-inch guns. A heavy hit was sustained below the waterline as *Prince of Wales* maneuvered through the wreckage of Hood. At 06:02, a 15-inch shell struck the starboard side of the compass platform and killed the majority of the personnel there. The navigating officer was wounded, but Captain Leach was unhurt. Casualties were caused by the fragments from the shell's ballistic cap and the material it dislodged in its diagonal path through the compass platform. A 15-inch diving shell penetrated the ship's side below the armour belt amidships, failed to explode and came to rest in the wing compartments on the starboard side of the after boiler rooms. The shell was only discovered and defused much later when the ship was docked at Rosyth. At 06:05 Captain Leach decided to disengage and laid down a heavy smokescreen to cover *Prince of Wales* escape. But not before scoring some damaging hits to the *Bismarck*'s fuel tanks. Kapitain Lindermann wanted to finish off *Prince of Wales* but was over-ruled by Admiral Lutjens. As he stated, "we are not here to attack the Royal Navy and should proceed with Exercise Rhine". 0629 Lutjen's received first damage reports.

0705 Winston Churchill awakes to hear of the loss of the *HMS Hood*. Winston Churchill was residing in the Prime Minister's County home of Chequers in Buckinghamshire, and he was entertaining William Averell Harriman, who served President Franklin D. Roosevelt as a special envoy to Europe later to become the US Ambassador to Britain. Churchill tells Harriman the depressing news. "They have sunk the Hood" "But this means WE'VE GOT THE BISMARCK!" 0755 Churchill sends this message to the Admiralty "I don't care how you do it, I don't care how many ships you use, but SINK THE BISMARCK!"

1230 Admiral Lutjens receives the serious damage reports from *Bismarck*'s engineers. It now became obvious that *Bismarck* needed a dry dock. Her fuel tanks on the starboard had been badly damaged and precious fuel was being replaced by sea water, even though her tanks were being balanced, she was now low in the bow. Lutjens realised that to take a broken *Bismarck* back to Germany would have been a complete embarrassment and a danger in transit. It was known that at St Nazaire in Bordeaux, there was a large dry dock built for the ocean liner "Normandy" which was large enough to take *Bismarck*. At 1240, Lutjens changed course and headed for France at 24 Knots. Meanwhile, the hunt was on, British ships were called from every area to intercept the *Bismarck*. Force H from Gibraltar, led by Admiral Somerville headed north with cruisers *HMS Renown*, *HMS* Sheffield and the aircraft carrier *HMS Ark Royal*. At a safe distance, keeping track, were cruisers, *Norfolk* and *Suffolk*. *Suffolk* would use her Radar to track and follow *Bismarck*. After some time, *Bismarck* sent a message to Group North control that she was unable to shake off the British ships due to their use of Radar. *Bismarck* slows down and turns her mighty 15 inch guns on the cruiser *Suffolk*. All shells missed, and *Bismarck* continued. At this stage, the British had no idea where *Bismarck* was heading. Again, *Bismarck* fires at *HMS Suffolk*. The damaged *HMS Prince of Wales* which was now back in the chase was working with *Suffolk*, and fires at *Bismarck*. However due to her turrets still malfunctioning *Prince of Wales* had to leave the theatre and returned home for repairs.

Meanwhile, Lutjens had decided that *Prinz Eugen* should continue with Exercise Rhine. It was arranged to part their ways as *Bismarck* would head to France for repairs. Now, I think that this was a liberty of the first degree. It was arranged that the two German ships would part when a particular code-word was sent. That code-word was "Hood". The signal was sent, and at 19.15, on the 24th May, the two German warships parted for the last time. As Lutjens knew he was being followed, he tried to lure the British ships into a U-boat trap, but due to a lack of fuel, this could not succeed. *Bismarck* was now heading directly to France.

Day 8

Sunday 25th May. 0015 *HMS Victorious* launches an attack on *Bismarck* by a fleet of Fairey Swordfish torpedo planes. These ancient-looking bi-planes looked as if they were left over from the First World War. Known as "String bags", they were actually built in the 1930s, and first used in 1934. They were designed to fly slow at 90mph, and could lay mines and carry torpedoes. Once the fleet of swordfish located *Bismarck*, they fired their torpedoes. They made several hits, but did no damage, owing to the 320mm thick armoured belt which protected *Bismarck*. One German sailor was killed due to severe vibration, but there was no other damage. The weather was now turning bad so all the Swordfish returned, bar one. The Swordfish would fly in very low to launch their torpedoes, which was the benefit of the low speed. The anti-aircraft guns on *Bismarck* were unable to aim at such a low angle. *Bismarck* fired shells into the water and the massive spray brought one Swordfish down. Visibility and weather were now both deteriorating even more and Lutjens decided to change course and shake off the British, once and for all.

0315 in extremely poor visibility, *Bismarck* turned 180 degrees starboard. It circled right around the rear of the British cruisers and for a short time, headed east. The maneuver worked and the British had now completely lost *Bismarck*. Dozens of British ships were now involved with the hunt. All British ships were now running low on fuel. *HMS Repulse* has to retire as she had virtually run dry. Lutjens wrongly believed that the British were still following him. At 0900, Lutjens sent a very long radio message of telling his headquarters at group west in Paris of the exact situation. Sending radio messages from a ship could easily give your position away. These signals were picked up by a high frequency direction-finding station (HFDF known as HUF-DUF).

Lutjens should have kept his radio signals to the bare minimum, he made a massive error. His signal lasted thirty-six minutes, which was picked up by the British. Though at that time, Bletchley Park were unable to decipher the message as *Bismarck* was using the "Hydra" code-book. Bismarck's position was signaled to Tovey but due to another serious error in *KG5's* plotting room, Tovey made a huge navigational miscalculation, he sent the British fleet in the wrong direction as he believed that *Bismarck* was on her way back to Germany. By the time he realised his mistake, the *Bismarck* was a day away and would soon have the protection of the *Luftwaffe* and U-boats.

We did make some observations. Lutjens changed *Bismarck's* control centre from Group North Wilhelmshaven, Germany to Group West Paris. Though Bletchley Park could not read Lutjens signal, he was located using Bletchley Park's traffic analysis system. We also were able to establish that he had asked for *Luftwaffe* air cover in the Biscay area for the Bismarck, as we were able to read *Luftwaffe* traffic this was hastily passed to the Admiralty. This gave the British the knowledge that *Bismarck* was in fact heading for France. Another observation was made, but in this instant there were delays at Bletchley Park with an unfortunate communication issue between Harry Hinsley and the Admiralty, therefore the information was too late to be of any use. A senior *Luftwaffe* officer General Hans Jeschonnek in command of planning in Greece got wind that the *Bismarck* was in trouble. He had a close relative onboard and wanted to find out the latest situation, so he sent a signal to his headquarters using his Enigma "Red code", which Bletchley Park were breaking on a daily basis. The message came back "Don't worry, the heavy ship (*Bismarck*) is heading to Brest in France not Norway".

The time this message reached Admiral Jack Tovey *Bismarck* had already been located. The 25th May 1941 was a special day for Admiral Lutjens, it was his birthday and at 0900 he received a greeting from Grand Admiral Raeder, and later in the day from Adolf Hitler (did they have a feeling it would be his last?). At 1145, Lutjens decided to speak to his crew. He wanted to motivate them as they had been told that their ship is the greatest in the world. But they were all aware that *Bismarck* was in trouble. So Lutjens spoke to his crew, and ended by telling them "it's victory or death", that must have cheered them up, no end.

Day 9

Monday May 26th 1941. 1030 Dennis Briggs, piloting a Catalina aircraft, using co-ordinates from direction-finding performed an arduous search. Just at a point where fuel was becoming an issue and the crew was thinking of returning empty handed, *Bismarck* was spotted. It must be mentioned that this was an American aircraft and crew, but the RAF pilot was British as America was not officially at war with Germany until the following December. Information of *Bismarck's* location gets back to Admiral Tovey onboard *HMS King George V.* Tovey now only had one option left, as all other ships steamed at full speed towards the location of the *Bismarck*, some on critical levels of fuel and that was to use the Swordfish torpedo planes.

1500 *Ark Royal* launched fifteen Swordfish torpedo aircraft. At 1610, they sighted what they believed was Bismarck, and dropped their torpedoes. However, they had made a grave error, they were attacking the wrong ship the *Sheffield*. The pilots apparently were not informed that *Sheffield* would be between *Ark Royal* and the *Bismarck*. Through a miracle and some quick action by the *Sheffield's* Captain, Charles Arthur Aiskew Larcom all torpedoes missed or exploded in the sea. It was also fortunate that the torpedoes involved had ineffective magnetic detonators.

1740 *HMS Sheffield,* part of Force H, located and shadowed *Bismarck*, 1910 Ark Royal launches another attack using torpedoes with direct contact detonators with the Swordfish biplanes.

At 2047 on 26th May *HMS Ark Royal*, part of H Force, sent further Swordfish to a relentless attack on *Bismarck* from various angles. Many torpedoes made hits, but once again, due to *Bismarck's* armoured belt, caused no real damage. Then, at 2105 a lucky hit by one torpedo struck *Bismarck's* aft. Many of the Swordfish planes were hit with anti-aircraft fire, one was hit 175 times but all planes returned to Ark Royal safely, but the despondent aircrews believed they failed in their mission. As it so happened that hit in *Bismarck's* aft struck her rudder which seriously damaged her steering gear. At 0930 *Sheffield* reports *Bismarck* sailing an erratic course.

The damage caused the rudder to become distorted and jammed at an angle 15° to port, which flooded the steering gear compartment. The effect was that *Bismarck* would go around in circles. *Bismarck*'s engineers and divers frantically attempted repairs, but to no avail. Lutjens ordered *Bismarck* to steer by using alternate propellers instead. This was virtually impossible, and the situation was futile. The British were now quite confused, as they saw *Bismarck* turn around and head towards them. They soon realised that *Bismarck* was having serious problems.

2140, Admiral Lutjens sent the report "Ship unable to maneuver, will fight to last shell. Long live the Fuehrer!" Admiral Tovey now surrounded *Bismarck* with British ships as they arrived on the scene. 23.58 *Bismarck* reported to Group West "Surrounded by enemy ships". Though British ships were spasmodically attacking throughout the night, Tovey decided that it would be better to leave any further action until daylight.

Day 10 of Exercise Rhine.

Tuesday 27th May 1941. 0500, *Bismarck* sent a weather report to Group West, hoping this would assist the promised *Luftwaffe* cover. 0625, *Bismarck* reported that the situation was unchanged. 0710, the last radio signals were sent from *Bismarck* "Send U-Boat for safekeeping of war diary". At 0840, Tovey signalled all of the ships in place, and at 0844, he sent a signal to them all "Finish her off" The battle commenced at 0845. The main attack came from the battleship *HMS Rodney* after some ranging salvos a direct hit knocked out *Bismarck*'s forward turrets "Anton & Bruno". 0908, other ships were now firing, fires broke out all over *Bismarck*'s decks. More British ships joined the battle, their shelling caused superstructure to fall on the crew. There were already many casualties, and then another direct hit by *HMS Rodney*, which knocked out the rear turrets ("Caesar and Dora"). 09.31, *Bismarck*'s main guns were now silenced, but her side guns were still firing. Massive fires and explosions were coming from below decks. There would be no sign of surrender from this pride of Germany's battleship. So the battle continued, and Lutjens had made it clear that they would fight until the last shell. But it appeared that there was an order to scuttle *Bismarck* before the British attempted to sink her. Detonators were set in the turbine rooms. Explosions soon followed. At 10.00

HMS Dorsetshire moved in and attacked with several mk VII torpedoes. At 1022 *Bismarck* rolled over onto one side, and Admiral Tovey could now see that *Bismarck* was finished, and called all ships off, as fuel was now at critical levels. *Dorsetshire* was left to finish the job. At 1037, *HMS Dorsetshire* launched her third 21 inch mark 7 torpedo, loaded with high quantities of extremely high explosive "Torpex", blasted a massive hole in the side of *Bismarck*'s hull, beneath her armoured belt. Then, at 10.39 on 27th May 1941, the mighty German battleship that bore the name of Germany's iron chancellor, rolled over 180° then sliped beneath the stormy Atlantic Ocean.

Winston Churchill's revenge for the sinking of the Royal Navy's pride *HMS Hood*, is complete. For *KMS Bismarck*, it was "Game Over". Now came the task of picking up the survivors. The *Bismarck* had a crew of 2,200, and preparations were made to pick up as many as possible. But there was a major problem: U-boats had been reported in the vicinity, which meant that all the British ships had to pull away. The danger of losing a British ship to a U-boat torpedo just could not be risked. All British ships were ordered to vacate the area immediately, leaving thousands of young German sailors to a watery grave. The Navy had a tradition once a ship was sunk, and providing the enemy sailors were of no threat, the prisoners would be treated well, as they were just sailors. So it was with great regret and sadness for the British sailors that we had to leave their potential prisoners to drown, in all 118 out of 2200 *Bismarck*'s crew were rescued.

In Staffordshire at the National Arboretum Memorial there is a special memorial to the British sailors lost on *HMS Hood* on 24th May 1941. In Germany, in the town of Friedrichsruhe, the home of Otto Von *Bismarck*, there is a memorial to the German sailors of KMS *Bismarck*, sunk on 27th May 1941. More recently, in 1989, Dr Robert Ballard used a remote controlled underwater vehicle, RUV, to search and locate the *Bismarck*. Dr Ballard has published a fantastic book containing many photographs of the sunken battleship *(Discovery of the Bismarck)* There are many books telling this fascinating story, including "*The Pursuit*" by Ludovic Kennedy, the journalist and news correspondent, who served as an officer onboard *HMS Tartar*, one of the sixty-four British and one Polish ship that were in this operation.

Even today Blohm & Voss are still operating in Hamburg, servicing ships and ferries using Dock 37, the very slipway that launched the *Bismarck*.

Summing up.

The lack of understanding of his navy was undoubtedly a part of Hitler's downfall. Hitler was a land commander, but in his position as General Commander in Chief, he should have taken an interest in the *Kriegsmarine* and its operations. He left it all to his Grand Admiral. Surely, for these massive battleships *Bismarck* and *Tirpitz* to prowl the Atlantic at will, was always going to be a great risk, as the Royal Navy would never allowed that kind of operation to succeed, it would just not have happened. Also, ignored by Hitler and lucky for the British was Admiral Doenitz's call that if he had the three hundred U-boats, that he had requested "he could bring Britain to her knees within five months" Another danger could have been the production of aircraft carriers, built but never completed, Hitler once said himself that on land he was a hero but at sea he was a coward. This certainly showed in Germany's failed "Operation Rhine".

Conclusion

KMS Bismarck was the wrong ship, at the wrong time, on the wrong day.

Ships involved

Battleships	x 5
Battle-cruisers	x 3
Aircraft carriers	x 2
Submarines	x 8
Cruisers	x 13
Destroyers	x 33

Home Fleet. 32

Battleship	King George V.	Scapa Flow
Battleship	Prince of Wales	Scapa Flow
Battleship	Rodney	En route from the Clyde to Boston with the troop transport ship *Britannic*
Battle Cruiser	Repulse	Clyde, assigned to troop convoyWS-8B
Battle Cruiser	Hood	Scapa Flow
Aircraft Carrier	Victorious	Scapa Flow, assigned to troop convoy WS-8B
Cruiser	Norfolk	Denmark Strait, on patrol
Cruiser	Suffolk	Refueling at Reykjavik, Iceland
Cruiser	Galatea	Scapa Flow
Cruiser	Aurora	Scapa Flow
Cruiser	Kenya	Scapa Flow
Cruiser	Neptune	Scapa Flow

Cruiser	Arethusa	En route to Reykjavik, Iceland
Cruiser	Edinburgh	Off the Azores, on patrol
Cruiser	Manchester	Faeroe Islands passage, on Patrol
Cruiser	Birmingham	Faeroe Islands passage, on Patrol
Destroyer	Inglefield	En route to Scapa Flow
Destroyer	Intrepid	En route to Scapa Flow
Destroyer	Active	Scapa Flow
Destroyer	Antelope	Scapa Flow
Destroyer	Achates	Scapa Flow
Destroyer	Anthony	Scapa Flow
Destroyer	Electra	Scapa Flow
Destroyer	Echo	Scapa Flow
Destroyer	Somali	At sea with Rodney and Britannic
Destroyer	Tartar	At sea with Rodney and Britannic
Destroyer	Mashona	At sea with Rodney and Britannic
Destroyer	Eskimo	At sea with Rodney and Britannic
Destroyer	Punjabi	Scapa Flow
Destroyer	Icarus	Scapa Flow
Destroyer	Nestor	Scapa Flow
Destroyer	Jupiter	Londonderry

Western Approaches Command. 6

Cruiser	Hermione	En route to Scapa Flow
Destroyer	Lance	Scapa Flow
Destroyer	Legion	Clyde, with battle cruiser Repulse
Destroyer	Saguenay	Clyde, with battle cruiser Repulse
Destroyer	Assiniboine	Clyde, with battle cruiser Repulse
Destroyer	Columbia	Londonderry

Plymouth Command, 4th Destroyer Flotilla. 5

Destroyer	Cossack	Clyde, assigned to troop Convoy WS-8B
Destroyer	Sikh	Clyde, assigned to troop convoy WS-8B
Destroyer	Zulu	Clyde, assigned to troop convoy WS-8B
Destroyer	Maori	Clyde, assigned to troop Convoy WS-8B
Destroyer (*Polish*) Piorun		Clyde, assigned to troop Convoy WS-8B

Nore Command 1

Destroyer	Windsor	Scapa Flow

Force H. 9

Battle Cruiser	Renown	Gibraltar
Aircraft Carrier	Ark Royal	Gibraltar
Cruiser	Sheffield	Gibraltar
Destroyer	Faulknor	Gibraltar
Destroyer	Foresight	Gibraltar
Destroyer	Forester	Gibraltar
Destroyer	Foxhound	Gibraltar
Destroyer	Fury	Gibraltar
Destroyer	Hesperus	Gibraltar

America and West Indies Station. 2

Battleship	Ramillies	At sea, escorting convoy HX-127
Battleship	Revenge	Halifax, Nova Scotia

South Atlantic Command. 1

Cruiser	Dorsetshire	At sea, escorting convoy SL-74

The following crafts were also deployed. 8

Submarine Minerva	On patrol off southwestern Norway
Submarine P-31	Scapa Flow
Submarine Sealion	English Channel

Submarine Seawolf	English Channel
Submarine Sturgeon	English Channel
Submarine Pandora	En route from Gibraltar to Great Britain
Submarine Tigris	Clyde
Submarine H-44	Rothesay

Exercise Rhine

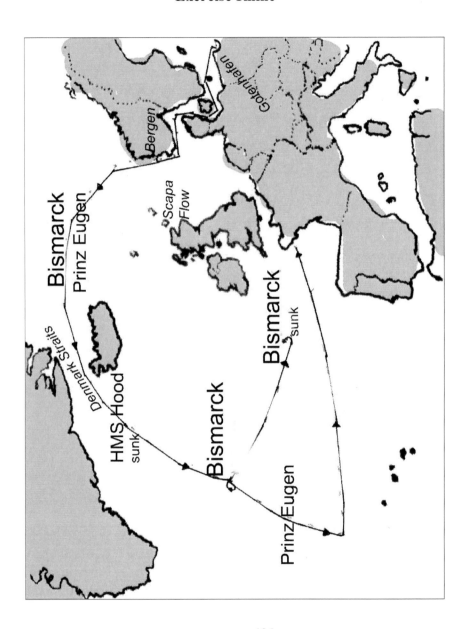

Battleship Tirpitz

Tirpitz was the second of Hitler's mighty battleships that he thought would help to bring Britain to its knees by commerce raiding in the north Atlantic, which he called "Plan Z". After the destruction of her sister ship Bismarck, Hitler ordered that she should not leave the Norwegian fjords where she was hiding for years.

While on station in Trondheim, Norway, the Royal Navy was committed to have many ships on standby in case *Tirpitz* tried to break out. In July 1942 there was a rumour that was based on bad intelligence at the British admiralty that *Tirpitz* was heading north to intercept and attack an Arctic convoy. Then the admiralty overreacted and this intern resulted with two-thirds of the Arctic convoy PQ 17 to be destroyed. However the truth was *Tirpitz* had not left her anchorage in the fjord. It was just a rumour.

Tirpitz only fired her big guns once in anger; in early September 1943 this was at a soft target, at an allied weather station on the island of Spitzbergen. The main purpose of this was to make a film for the German ministry of propaganda, to show the power of the German navy.

Tirpitz was continually attacked by the RAF since the early days of her construction. There were no direct hits, but it did slow down her build, which prevented Bismarck and *Tirpitz* to become operational at the same time. The initial plan was for these two massive battleships to operate together as one major threat in the north Atlantic to destroy British food convoys.

25th September 1943 *Tirpitz* was attacked by Royal Navy X craft midget submarines (Operation Source) which caused substantial damage and put her out of action until April 1944. Repairs were carried out on site by a German maintenance ship. Further attacks followed over the months from the RAF causing few hits and minimal damage. Eventually *Tirpitz* was moved to her last final anchorage in Tromso fjord.

A Norwegian resistance worker operating a secret radio transmitter reported back to London *Tirpitz* position. On the 12th of November 1944 she was attacked by the Lancaster aircrafts of the RAF number 9 and number 617 squadrons. They dropped 29 x 12,000 pound Tallboy bombs. Two bombs hit their target, but only one detonated causing a large rip in her superstructure. One bomb landed in the Fjord and exploded in the shingle. The massive shock wave caused *Tirpitz* to capsize. The locals now remember stories of the people of that day, telling that they were hearing banging on the inside of the upturned hull for several days after. Holes were cut to release some of the crew but after a time you could hear the remaining trapped crew singing Deutschland, Deutschland über alles" and then silence.

1,204 out of 2,065 officers and men perished on the Tirpitz. After the war Tirpitz was cut up for scrap by German and Norwegian Companies. By 1957 the vast majority was removed but still large parts of the *Tirpitz* remain buried in the gravel in Tromso Fjord to this day that will probably never be removed.

In 2015 the author visited the *Tirpitz* museum on the banks of Tromso fjord. The ships Enigma machine including other remains are exhibited close to where the 58000 ton fully laden Battleship *Tirpitz*, which never sank another ship, was sunk.

Spies Lies and Double Cross Agents

Spies.

When you think of a spy what is conjured up in your mind? Possibly two men in trilby hats, whispering secrets to each in a dark corner or alleyway, or maybe you think of Ian Fleming's allegedly covert agent 007? I always find it strange that we call our secret agents, agents. Foreign agents we call spies. Spies have to remain invisible, no one should be able to tell who they are. In the case of agent 007 James Bond everybody knows who he is. He can walk into any bar in the world. The barman will say "ahh!" Mr Bond we've been expecting you. The barman will then proceed to pour James Bond his favourite cocktail shaken and not stirred. So what does a spy really look like? If you look at an audience in the theatre or observe people at a bus stop or in a crowd that's exactly what spies look like. Like you and me ordinary everyday people. We will be looking at some ordinary people of the 1940s who played such an important role spying supposedly for the Germans but feeding them so much disinformation that it helped to form the foundations to which lead to operation overlord which had such a successful outcome.

The year is 1943, the Battle of the Atlantic is slowly being won. Up to now we had been losing the war. The German U-boats were sinking more of our merchant vessels then we were able to replace. In 1942 Britain needed to import 70% of its food and 95% of its oil, to survive. But only a fraction of this was being achieved, by that August Britain had six weeks supplies of food left. Food rationing was at its height. By late 1942 we had suffered the heaviest losses of merchant shipping in the war, 5.5 million tons in just ten months. The Bletchley Park code-breakers had just got back into the U-boat code "shark" which we were not able to break since February 1942. We could not afford to lose the code again. We were sinking U-boat at a higher frequency than ever before. We had to protect Ultra, which was the output product of Bletchley Park. Ultra was being used by the Royal air force with the help of Air to Surface Vessel radar (ASV) to locate U-boats and sink them. This was now more efficient than ever.

To protect Ultra and to avoid the Germans thinking we had compromised the Enigma code, British double agent Zigzag, one Eddie Chapman, through his German spymaster convinced Admiral Karl Doenitz commander of the U-boats that we had a new secret weapon. Agent Zigzag through his contacts supplied the Germans with fake plans and information about real factories that can produce this non existant weapon. The Germans believed that this weapon that could be launched off the side of a ship, similar to a torpedo. This weapon named SQID a notional version of the actual weapon of the same name, would by the use of electronics and sonar chase U-boats many hundreds of metres underwater until it made contact and detonated, eventually punching a hole in the side of the U-boat and sinking it. The Germans were so concerned about this new underwater weapon which did not exist, that they ordered their U-boats where ever possible sail on the surface of the Atlantic, which they obeyed without question. This obviously made easy pickings for our bombers to destroy the U-boats. By May 1943 Admiral Doenitz had lost over 100 U-boats. Even Doenitz own son was lost as one of the crew on a U-boat. By May 1943 owing to these severe loses Doenitz decided that it was time to remove the U-boats from the North Atlantic. They were sent to Norway to attack the Arctic convoys or down to patrol Mediterranean. Now the North Atlantic was becoming a safer place. It was time to start bringing equipment and personnel from the United States for the largest invasion that the world has ever known. "Operation Overlord" the reclaiming of Europe. This is just one example how the disinformation passed to the Germans from the double agents changed the course of the war.

In early 1943 Winston Churchill and President Roosevelt had a meeting in Casablanca. It was time to discuss the war's end game. At this meeting tentative plans were made how the Allies would invade and liberate Europe and rid it of the Nazi regime. Later that year another meeting was held at Tehran where Churchill, Roosevelt and Stalin discussed the different options for diversionary plans. The general invasion was almost certainly going to be at the Normandy beaches. We had to make the Germans believe it was going to be elsewhere. The Germans knew that sooner or later the allies would attempt some kind of operation. The Germans also knew there would be some kind of diversionary raid. So the plan was to organise many diversions to really confuse the Germans. This would involve very subtle and totally select planning. Winston Churchill said "this whole affair must be protected by a bodyguard of lies".

The overall diversion plan was called "Operation Bodyguard." The plans for this would be made by the London controlling section. Made up of a committee of top military personnel from all the services including MI5 and MI6 there were also members of the war cabinet. The British intelligence services would play a major role in this deception planning operation. It is MI5 who are responsible for home security, defense of the realm and MI6 who looked at threats from overseas and deploying agents in foreign lands. The wireless intercept service was also involved (*Y Service*) these were our ears on Europe, intercepting enemy messages. Bletchley Park would be deciphering the coded signals from the Y-stations then passing them on to the British military Headquarters. The radio security service, run jointly by the General Post Office (GPO) and MI5, was Listing out for clandestine radio transmissions from inside Britain. They were assisted by hundreds of amateur radio operators who acted as voluntary interceptors (VI's). The most important help that we had come from the German defense agency themselves known as the *Abwehr*.

Abwehr

Controlled by Admiral Wilhelm Franz Canaris born in 1887, who worked as an intelligence officer in the Imperial German Navy during the First World War. During the 1930s he became a commanding officer of the battleship *Schlesien.* When Hitler came to power Canaris never agreed with the Nazis, nevertheless he was promoted by them to Admiral status, to the head of the German defense agency the *Abwehr.* Canaris only employed the minimum Nazi members he could get away with, to keep Himler at bay. Canaris always supported Germany as he considered himself as an Admiral of the German Imperial Navy (his belief). Eventually he fell foul of Hitler and was sacked. The *Abwehr* was disbanded and taken over by the SD (*Sicherheitsdienst*) the intelligence agency of the SS a sister organisation of the Gestapo. The *Abwehr* tended to believe all the information that we sent to them via our double agents without question. They passed the information on to the *Abwehr* headquarters in Hamburg then onto the *Fremde Herre West* FHW who were the collators of all German intelligence, forwarded again to chiefs of staff at the *Oberkommando* Der *Wehrmacht* in Berlin which was directed to the desk of Adolf Hitler himself. Hitler failed to disbelieve any of this fabricated information that we wanted him to have.

The *Abwehr* would send spies to Britain. They would be either dropped in by parachute into a remote field somewhere or they would be put off a boat or submarine close to the British coast, into a dinghy, then row to shore to a remote cove. Spies also came into Britain posing as one of the many refugees escaping Nazi Germany. Once in Britain the spy would find a hidden area and make radio contact with their handlers. Their message would be converted into a hand cipher stating their safe arrival. The radio set was supplied with plug-in crystals that were tuned to a fixed frequency. A specific time would have been allocated to transmit the message The spies message was then received by the *Abwehr* handler who would possibly be in Paris, Madrid, Lisbon or even Oslo. The message would be checked then converted into an unreadable cipher using the G type Enigma machine then sent on by radio Morse code. This was then received at *Abwehr* radio headquarters in Hamburg. Eventually this was forwarded on to Berlin.

Soon as the German spies in Britain made their first radio transmission it was very quickly intercepted by our radio security service through either the voluntary interceptors or by our direction finding systems. Spies were tracked down very quickly and arrested. The Radio Security Service (RSS) headquarters were initially set up jointly by MI5 and the General Post Office (GPO) to locate and intercept clandestine radio transmissions mainly from within Britain. A member of British naval intelligence Arthur Watts was one of the founder members of the RSS, was also a keen radio amateur and president of the radio Society of Great Britain. The RSS would be initially located in dingy offices accommodated in spare cells at Wormwood Scrubs prison in West London. As the war progressed they moved to a safer haven outside London at Arkley View Barnet Hertfordshire. This was a large house with a row of typically temporary government huts in the rear garden. The RSS headquarters in Barnet was simply known as PO Box 25 Barnet. It was soon realised that the handful of intercept stations around the country sending their messages to PO Box 25 were grossly insufficient, for the amount of radio traffic coming across the airways. A Arthur Watts approached the Radio Society of Great Britain (RSGB), to contact thousands of their members who were amateur radio operators (radio hams) who at the commencement of the war had their radio transmitters confiscated. The radio hams were allowed to keep their radio receiving equipment. Where operators were not of the military age or were disabled they were contacted and asked to become voluntary interceptors (VI's). They were thoroughly checked out and had to sign the Official Secrets Act. Their job would be to scan the airways searching for unexplained radio transmissions normally in code. Once located the details would be entered on a RSS log sheet and sent by post to PO Box 25 Barnet. At Arkley View they would collate all the information. It would be sent through to Bletchley Park for the messages to be deciphered and sent back to MI5. PO Box 25 were now receiving thousands of messages every day. Many of them commercial legitimate messages, Others were from possible German agents. These agents/spies had to be tracked down very quickly. It appeared that some of the VI's were attempting to decode messages themselves. This practice was immediately made illegal as this could undermine this whole security operation. PO Box 25 now completely run by MI5 grew out of its efficiency due to high levels of work in coming. To maintain further security an approach was made to Brigadier Richard Gambier Parry chief of MI6 section 8 communications. He was asked to set up a new home for the RSS in North Bucks just 10 miles north of Bletchley Park at a location called Hanslope Park. This became known as special communications unit three (SCU3) Gambier Parry was also responsible for Whaddon Hall 4 miles to the west of Bletchley Park known as SCU1 where disseminated decoded military signals from Bletchley Park known as Ultra were forwarded by radio to our commanders in the theatres of war.

Bletchley Park the home of the Government Code and Cipher School had many functions in wartime signals intelligence, hence the 10,000 staff that eventually worked for the establishment. One of the code-breaker's tasks was to break into the German spy network. There are two sides to this operation. The radio security service now at Hanslope Park will pass to Bletchley Park the intercepted signals from the German agents that had entered Britain. The agent would have been signaling to their handler or controller in Lisbon or Madrid etc he/she would be using a hand cipher. This code was broken by Oliver Strachey at Bletchley Park who was a veteran code-breaker from World War I's military section called MI1b this information was passed to MI5 that told us where the enemy agent is located. Where he is going and what he has observed, also when he will make his next radio transmission. This information was passed to MI5 which enabled them to quickly locate and arrest the spy. The spymaster or controller in Lisbon or Madrid would send the message which was received from the German agent in Britain, to the *Abwehr* radio headquarters in Hamburg. To send this message the information would be encoded on to the Enigma cipher machine these signals were intercepted by our wireless intercept stations "Y" stations, these were located mainly around the coast of Britain. Signals went directly to Bletchley Park's Registry to be sorted then passed to the relevant code-breaking dept. Alfred Dillwyn Knox (Dilly Knox) the chief code-breaker who was also a veteran code-breaker from World War 1 Knox worked for the Naval Intelligence Department 25 at room 40 at the Old Admiralty buildings in London. Now at Bletchley Park, Knox had broken the *Abwehr* Enigma early in the war which gave MI5 a deep insight to the complete workings of the German defense agency.

As soon as the German agents were located, a welcoming party from the police and MI5 made an arrest very quickly. Camp 020 which was the interrogation camp for all German agents who were arrested as spies or who volunteered their services as a German spy working for Britain as a double agent. Camp 020 was situated at Latchmere house near to Richmond in surrey. The camp commandant was Lt Col Robin Stevens. His methods of interrogation were never violent. He could fiercely stare at the suspect with such ferocity that they would speak quite freely, frightened as to what their fate would be. Stevens was known as "old tin eye Stevens" who could put the fear of God into them.

German agents fell into three main categories: stupid, loyal, or mercenary. The stupid spy was badly selected by the *Abwehr*. He had no chance of surviving in this environment and was probably forced into spying through some kind of threat. These were put into prison for the rest of the war. If the spy was a loyal supporter of Hitler and the Nazi regime they would be tried and executed. Then you had the mercenary. These are the ones that did it for the money, the lifestyle, the buzz, and the sheer thrill of being a spy. These were the most important to us as we would possibly turn these spies to work for Britain. If they were clever they could be paid by the *Abwehr* and also MI5. These were known as double-agents. This situation caused an issue in our security services. Up until now, German spies were dealt with by MI5, who were responsible for home security. To consider these spies to act as our own agents would become the responsibility of MI6 the organisation who dealt with our agents overseas. So major discussions took place, it was decided that a new sub-organisation of MI5 would be created. To be set up by Thomas Argyll Robertson, known as "TAR", he was already a Case Officer for a British double agent "Snow", he now was to expand this subdivision.

MI5 B1a

At MI5 department B1a was set up to allow the control of double agents. A working group was to be chaired by John Cecil Marsterman (an Oxford don, and writer of thrillers). It was to become the Twenty Committee, named after the two crosses (double *cross*) representing the Roman twenty "XX". They met once a week at 58 St James's St London SW1. MI5 Department B1a was now responsible for all Double Cross activities. When an enemy spy arrived in Britain, they were equipped with the following: radio transmitter, invisible ink, code-book, revolver, wad of cash and a pill containing Potassium Cyanide and a questionnaire.

The questionnaire consisted of a list of what the Germans wanted their spy to find out, and to send the information back to them by radio or letter written with secret ink. This information could be regarding the sighting and whereabouts of troops, information about dockyards or factories, even the problems caused by bomb damage or public opinion. So once a spy was caught, and providing he was suitable as a double agent, he needed to respond to the Germans' questionnaire. So this was our opportunity to give false information to the Germans. This obviously had to be a very subtle operation so not to cause the Germans to believe that their agent was being controlled by the British.

Yet another department was set up. Known as the wireless board "W Board", they would create the information that we wanted the Germans to believe, their input came from the military and our security services. The W board would add to the fabrication was some true information that would be harmless for the enemy to have to give it the air of authenticity. This was known as "Chicken feed", the double agent would then send that information back to their *Abwehr* handlers in Madrid or Lisbon, using their radio set. The message was sent using the *Abwehr* hand cipher, at a precise time and from the agent's location normally from an MI5 safe house. You could of course ask "how did we know if the agent is sending the exact message that we ordered them to send", as they may be acting as a triple agent. Or is it possible that the spy was given a secret control character to send within the message that would indicate that the agent is being controlled by the British. What the agent did not know and was not going to find out was that not only was their radio transmission monitored between London and their handling agents, it was also being tracked from the handling agents to *Abwehr* HQ in Hamburg. So we knew that the Germans were trusting all of the information we were sending to them, which was believed whole heartedly right to the very top of the Third Reich. This was the basis of how the deception plans for D Day were to be created.

I have chosen five spies who were key in delivering the main source of fabricated chicken feed, getting to the very top of the Third Reich which enforced their belief of the of the deception plans that the allies were intent on using for the invasion of Europe, hopefully, once and for all to rid Europe of the Nazi menace. These five spies, through one reason or another volunteered their services to British Intelligence while pretending to work for the Germans. One mistake would have cost them and possibly their families lives and could have probably blown the plan for D-Day, which then could have delayed victory for years, at a terrible cost.

Dusko Popov:

Dusko Popov was the Yugoslavian, son of a very wealthy businessman with contacts in high places. Popov studied at Frieburg University. Whilst there, he had a friend who like himself, was also wealthy, Johnny Jebson. One day, Popov was out with his girlfriend in a restaurant, when the Gestapo arrested them both. Unbeknownst to Popov, she was being followed. He was not aware that she was an active Communist. The result being they were both thrown in gaol? Popov was treated badly. Through his father's personal business contacts with Herman Goering, Popov was released, but always maintained a hatred of the Nazis.

Some years later, his old friend from University, Johnny Jebson made contact and then agreed to meet up in a restaurant in Belgrade. Jebson put a proposition to Popov: "How would you like to make some money and have some fun?" Jebson continued "I work for the German Defense agency, the *Abwehr*. If you become my agent, we can both make some money." Popov agreed, that he would be prepared to spy for Germany (he was lying) probably for the fun more than the money. Jebson arranged for Popov to go to Lisbon and meet up with Kramer von Auenrode alias Ludovico von Karsthoff, who was to become Popov's handler. But prior to his journey and after his meeting with Johnny Jebson, Popov decided to contact the British Embassy in Belgrade. He was put in touch with an agent who took notes and made special arrangements. Popov was then advised to continue with his contact in Lisbon.

Once in neutral Lisbon, he would be able to travel to Britain which was relatively easy, as there were reasonably regular flights. After his meeting with von Karsthoff, where he was trained in the art of spying, he was sent to England. Von Karsthoff gave him money, a questionnaire, and eventually, a radio set, this was Popov's license to have a great time on Nazi money.

As soon as Popov arrived in England, he checked into the Savoy Hotel in London, he made contact with the security services who had been tipped off by Belgrade. This is where he had an initial meeting with TAR Robertson, after several days of questions and interrogation TAR was satisfied with Popov's authenticity.

Popov was to operate under the control of MI5 dept. Belgrade B1a. He was allocated a case officer, Billy Lake. Popov's questionnaire from the Germans was given to the "W" board to fabricate answers to be sent back to them. The information would be sent to von Karsthoff by mail, written in invisible secret ink. Popov would be sent money in return, as well as another questionnaire. As far as Popov was concerned, "Let the good times roll!" Gambling, booze, girls and fun fun fun! Yes, all this in the middle of World War II After some time of hoodwinking the enemy, came a request from the Germans. They said as Popov was so successful in Britain, and sending all this reliable *notional* information back to Germany, "We would like you to go to the USA to set up the same kind of operation." The orders involved starting up a network of agents. Popov was not too happy about this as he was having such a great time. British Intelligence suggested that if he did not go, they may suspect that he was being controlled by the British. MI5 B1a contacted the FBI which was run by J. Edgar Hoover. Hoover did not want any German spies in America. He said "the only thing we do with German spies is shoot them." But orders came from above and in August 1941, Popov travelled to USA to spy for the Germans (in theory). When Popov viewed his list of questions of what the German wanted to know, they were very keen to know about bases in Hawaii especially Pearl Harbour. This information was filtered back via MI5 onto J. Edgar Hoover, but either this was not taken seriously or was not passed on. Just four months later, in December 1941, Japan attacked Pearl Harbour causing untold damage and bringing the US into the war. It looks apparent that the Americans were forewarned but did very little.

For Popov, once again, it was business as usual, time to have more fun with Hitler's money, it was spend spend spend! When he ran out of money, he asked the Germans for more cash, which they sent. When the Germans refused to send anymore Popov borrowed and ran up massive debts. He gambled, had many girlfriends, bought expensive motor cars, and made himself a playboy, a menace and a nuisance. Hoover was fed up hearing about his escapades, and ordered him out of the country or "he would have him arrested, charged under the Man Act and thrown in jail".

Popov returned to Lisbon. On his return von Karsthoff was not well pleased and had ordered Popov to attend a meeting so that he could question him on why the USA operation failed to produce any new agents. Popov immediately took an offensive position by blaming the Germans for not sending him enough money, and wasting his valuable time by under-funding the operation. Popov said, "I have a good mind to resign over your failure to finance the operation correctly". Now, Popov was not stupid, he knew that a lot of the monies coming from German for agents like himself were being creamed off by the handlers like von Karsthoff. He found this out from his friend Johny Jebsen, who was always on the fiddle. If von Karsthoff was caught creaming off agents' money, he would be sent to Berlin and possibly interviewed by the Gestapo then if lucky, sent the Russian Front! So Popov got an immediate apology from von Karsthoff who then asked if he could possibly return to England to carry on where he left off. Of course, this was accepted. Popov continued his "work" with MI5 B1a. Dusko Popov, MI5 agent "Tricycle" (due to an apparent preference of three in a bed), became our first D-day spy.

Roman Czerniawski

Czerniawski was a Polish Air force Officer and a hero. In 1940 he volunteered for allied espionage work in France. On day in a café in a quiet street in Paris he met up with Mathilde Carre. Mathilde also hated the Nazis together they decided to do something about it. They recruited agents for an organisation which they named "Interallie" (*Allied*). They were supplying information to the French resistance groups from their office in Montmartre in Paris. Their brilliant communications system involved placing messages in the toilets of railway coaches. By unscrewing the mirrors and placing the message behind. They became very successful with many agents all over France. One day, when he returned to the office, Czerniawski thought he recognised a man walking past him. It happened to be Hugo Bliecher of the *Abwehr*, who was working on behalf of the Gestapo.

The next thing they knew, on the 17th November 1941, was that the building was raided by the Gestapo. All the staff at "Interrallie" were arrested, and all their records were confiscated. The offices were trashed, and all the staff, including Czerniawski and Carre were arrested and thrown in a terrible Gestapo prison in Paris. Czerniawski as you can imagine was very badly treated, and was interrogated several times. On one occasion he was taken from his cell, and thought that he was going to be shot, but he was interrogated again, this time by a member of the *Abwehr*, Hugo Bliecher. They were quite impressed with how he had set up the organisation "Interallie".

The *Abwehr* gave him an option to set up as their agent in England and recruit more spies to work for the Germans and of course as he was Polish he could be accepted in Britain. The offer was one of those that he was unable to refuse. In other words, he was work as a spy for the Germans or be executed by them. Czerniawski agreed to spy for the *Abwehr* as it was his "get out of gaol free card". There was one caveat: The Germans made it clear that, in case he was thinking of double-crossing them, they knew where his family lived in Poland, and they would be in great peril. Roman Cziernaiwski was sent to England as a German agent. He immediately made his way to the Polish Embassy and was treated like a hero. He was then put in touch with the British Intelligence Services, and sent to camp 020 Latchmere House for interrogation by "Tin-Eye" Stevens, then handed over to MI5 B1a, and became our second D-day spy. His code-name was "Brutus", as he was to stab the Germans in the back.

Lily Sagayew

Nathalie "Lily" Sergueiew was born in St Petersburg, Russia in 1912. She escaped the Russian revolution in 1917, and reached France with her family. Lily was educated in Paris, trained as a journalist and could speak fluent English and German. During 1930, she travelled throughout Germany, interviewing top Nazis such as Herman Goering. In 1937, Lily was approached to work for German Intelligence. In this instance, she refused. After the fall of France in May 1940, she agreed to work for the *Abwehr*. Her case officer or Handler was Emil Kliemann.

Major Emile Kliemann of the German *Abwehr* was having a most delightful war. Occupied Paris was an exceptionally pleasant place to be, if you happened to sympathise with the Nazis. He had an office on the Champs-Élysées, a comfortable apartment near the Bois de Boulogne, Kliemann was two hours late for their rendezvous at the Café du Rond-Point. The young woman waiting at the corner table was goodlooking without being beautiful. In fluent German, Lily Sergeyev explained that she was a journalist and painter. Lily was intrigued, intelligent, and most important, interested in Kliemann. He invited her to dinner at the Cascade restaurant, near the Bois de Boulogne. The young woman insisted on bringing her dog, a small white male terrier-poodle cross named Babs, to which she was obviously devoted. Emil Kliemann trained Lily in intelligence techniques such as writing in secret ink, information gathering, and communications.

In May 1943, Lily travelled to Spain. She travelled everywhere with her beloved little dog. When Lily arrived in Madrid, she contacted British Intelligence at the passport office of the British embassy. British Embassy passport offices were nearly always a cover for MI6 to base their agents. Lily offered her services to British Intelligence. They accepted her and she was initially sent to Gibraltar to await transport to Britain. The authorities would not allow her to take her little dog with her due to the strict quarantine rules in the UK. Lily was very upset over this, but she was promised that they would look after the dog, and it would follow later. When she arrived in Britain, she was taken eventually to Rugby Mansions in Kensington, West London, where TAR Robertson interviewed her and introduced Lily to her British Handler Mary Shearer. What Lily was not aware of was her house-keeper A Yugoslavian woman Maritza was an MI5 agent "Snark" Keeping an eye on Lily, and reporting back on her movements. Lily started sending back information to Germany as Kliemann had provided Lily with a questionnaire. But Lily was depressed and became difficult for MI5 to control her. She was missing her dog badly and kept asking when it would arrive in England. The answer was always the same: soon. Lily continued to meet Kliemann by travelling back and forth to Lisbon, bringing back further questionnaires, but still no dog. Lily was becoming even more depressed, then a telegram from Gibraltar. "Your dog was sent to a kennel in Algiers and by complete accident it escaped from its cage and ran into a road, and was run over. We are very sorry.". Lily was convinced that the British killed her dog, and she wanted revenge. Lily was distraught and took it upon herself to make an arrangement with Kliemann that should she become controlled by the British, she would send certain hidden characters in her messages. This would have indicated that Lily was sending false information back to the *Abwehr*, which of course, she was. The information about the false character should have immediately been reported to MI5, but Lily kept it to herself so she could get revenge for the loss of her dog at any time.

Though she often thought about using it Lily never used the control signal to alert the Germans that she was being controlled by the British. She revealed her secret by chance to MI5, and they were livid that she was sitting on a time bomb. At any moment she could have wrecked the complete Double Cross system along with all the D-day planning. Lily was used for the build up to D-day, passing false information back to the Germans. But after D-day, she was sacked from MI5. But MI5 were still sending the Germans false information pretending it was coming from Lily Sergeyev, her code-name was "Treasure" because she really was, but at most times not. Lily became our third D-day spy.

Elvira de la Fuente Chaudior

Our next spy was the daughter of a very wealthy Peruvian,she was living in Paris, where she had spent most of her upbringing. Her father became Peruvian Charge d'affair to the Vichy government. Elvira got bored with everything she did in life. She even got married to a very wealthy businessman and got bored with him, and divorced. She moved to England and continued her high life there, with the night-clubs and gambling casinos, where Elvira always lost money. She could often be seen at Crockfords or Hamiltons Club in London's fashionable Mayfair. But eventually, she ran out of money. One night at Hamiltons, she was pouring out her misery over a Bronx cocktail to the sympathetic ear of an RAF officer. Elvira explained how bored she was, and now with no money. The RAF officer advised her that he could put her in touch with British Intelligence, where she could possibly find work and certainly not get bored. Elvira agreed, she was put in touch with Claude Damsey, the deputy Head of MI6, also with Duff Cooper, the Minister of Information.

There was an initial meeting set up at the Connaught Hotel in Mayfair. With her father's diplomatic status, it was relatively easy for Elvira to get into Vichy France, which was the capital of central and Southern part of France which after the German invasion of May 1940 remained under French control. In charge of Vichy Government was Philip Petain, a French WW1 hero, but unfortunately, now just a puppet for the Germans until they capitulated in November 1942. Elvira eventually got to France under the control of MI5 to continue her gambling in the exclusive clubs and casinos in Paris. She was still losing big time, but now it was MI5's money going around the roulette tables and down the drain. It was in one of these casinos that a friend of a friend put her in touch with someone who could provide Elvira with the money that she needed to throw at the tables. This someone happened to be Helmut Bleil, a freelance agent working as an *Abwehr* handler looking out for new recruits. Bleil gave Elvira the rundown of what would be expected of her, how she would have to go to Britain with a questionnaire and provide the Germans with information. Elvira was trained in communications, how to write letters in secret ink, and how to operate a radio transmitter. Bleil made it quite clear to Elvira that if she cheated on the Germans, it would cost her her life. Her German code-name was "Dorette". Bliel then handed Elvira a bottle of secret ink. As she put it in her handbag, she prayed that it would not clink on the other bottle of secret ink that MI5 had given her. Elvira made her way to Britain, and to work for MI5 B1a, she was handled by Hugh Astor. It would add the thrill to her life that she desperately needed to become Britain's fourth D-day spy, code-named "Bronx", the name of her favourite cocktail.

Bronx Cocktail Recipe

1 ½ ounces gin,
¼ ounce dry vermouth,
¼ ounce sweet vermouth,
1 ounce orange juice,
Orange slice for garnish.

Juan Pujol Garcia

In Spain it is traditional to take the father's surname after the Christian name and the mothers surname last. So as far as we are concerned he will be called Pujol. Pujol was not just a Catalonian chicken farmer, he had many jobs. He also served the army in the Spanish Civil war. He claimed to have fought on both sides without ever firing a bullet.

He hated war, he hated the communists, and equally hated the Fascists. When World War II broke out, Spain remained neutral, but it leaned relatively heavily on the side of Germany with an incredible network of active *Abwehr* agents. Pujol could see the Fascists, as in the Nazis, on the move again. He wanted to do anything he could to help the allies.

Pujol made contact with British intelligence via the British Passport office in Madrid. He attempted to offer his services to the British Intelligence as he could travel relatively freely being a respected businessman. However, after several approaches to MI6 he was sent away empty-handed. Pujol then figured out that if he could join the German intelligence service, he could supply them with false information. This he thought would be his contribution for helping the allies. Pujol's next call was to the office of the Madrid *Abwehr*, there he made contact with Gustav Leisner the head of the Madrid section. He told them that he was able to go to England and spy for the Germans. They said that it was a good idea and waved goodbye to him. He then asked for expenses to take him to England. They told him "Bring us back the information and then we will pay you" It seemed as if he was not taken seriously and once again he was given the cold shoulder.

Pujol then left their offices feeling dejected. A few days later he returned to the *Abwehr* office to play a very dangerous game with the Germans. He told them that he had come up with a plan. He showed them that he had been given a diplomatic passport by the Spanish authorities (this was a forgery) as they wanted him to go to England as an honorary Spanish attaché. This would enable him to travel freely to Britain and act as a German agent. Pujol also told the *Abwehr* that he knew a pilot and for a small fee he would take Pujol's reports / letters from England and post them to Madrid from a Lisbon Post Office. This in effect would by-pass the British censors. The Abwerh who believed every word of his ridiculous lies asked" how can we send you our questionnaires and payments" so Pujol gave the address of a friend in Lisbon as a cover address. In return the *Abwehr* gave Pujol a cover address in Madrid. So who at the Madrid *Abwehr* was responsible for believing all this nonsense? Head of section Gustav Leisner, Case Officer Karl-Erich Kuhlenthal, or Officer Friedrich Knappe-Ratey.

Instead of travelling to England Pujol and his family moved to Lisbon as soon as he was settled he headed down the road to a secondhand bookshop. He bought some English magazines, some old newspapers and a well-thumbed copy of the Blue Guide to Britain, along with viewing newsreels, agent "Arabel" (*his German code-name*) started to fabricate reports and send them to the *Abwehr* office in Madrid. Even Pujol was surprised when he was paid for these reports, the more he wrote, the more they paid. Pujol was virtually writing out his own cheques. This went on for many months. The *Abwehr*'s Lisbon case officer for Agent Arabel was Kuhlenthal. He would send this information onto *Abwehr* HQ in Hamburg and then onto the head of the Third Reich. Pujol was making big errors in his reports that the Germans never picked up on.

He was pretending to be travelling to Britain, spying for the Germans at Dockyards, ports and factories. The fact was that he never left Lisbon. Pujol was purporting to pay a pilot for posting his letters, he actually posted them himself and then pocketed the expenses, as if they came from Britain by aeroplane. He told the Germans that on his visit to Glasgow that he saw shipbuilders in cafes drinking flagons of wine. This error was never picked up by the Germans. He was also informing them of imaginary convoys leaving Liverpool for the Mediterranean, with the numbers of merchant ships and Royal Navy Convoy escort details. However, all this information was being paid for by the Germans, and then transmitted to the *Abwehr* HQ by radio, using the Enigma Cipher System. These messages were being intercepted and broken by Bletchley Park. The information was going back to MI5 B1a, who were then in a bit of a quandary. It appeared that there was a German agent called Arabel, operating in Britain about whom they knew nothing. The Radio Security Service (RSS) were put on full alert to listen out for signals from a German agent operating in Britain. As we believed it should not have been possible with the systems MI5 had in place. On closer inspection of the messages sent by Arabel, they just did not make any sense. Army camps where there were no army camps, factories where there were no factories, and convoys of ships that just didn't exist. What was going on? It was soon established that this information was coming via Madrid. MI6 agents were allocated to track down this mysterious spy. Eventually after several months, MI6 were able to locate agent Arabel operating from Lisbon. After interviews and interrogations, Juan Pujal Garcia and his family were secretly brought to Britain. The family were taken to an MI5 safe house at 35 Crespigny Road Cricklewood in North London.

After further interrogations by MI5, it was decided that, as he was such a good actor who could fool the Germans as he did so often, MI5 named him Garbo, after the actress Greta Garbo. He continued his work of supplying the Germans with false information. MI5 allocated him his British case officer Tommy Harris, a half Spanish art dealer who lived in Chelsea. Garbo's information was now composed for him by the W. Board (Wireless board), based on the questionnaires the German's were sending him. So now Garbo was being paid by MI5 (although not much) as well as receiving good money from the Germans. It was not long before Garbo started recruiting agents to spy for him. In time, he had set up a vast network of agents around Britain. They included Welsh fascists, lorry drivers, an army officer, dock workers, Gibraltarians, a South African Working at the Ministry of Information, employers of airlines, anti-Communists.

The Garbo network consisted of twenty-six sub-agents around the country, who all sent in intelligence reports to the Germans. The *Abwehr* in return were supplying Garbo with cash to pay all of his twenty six agents and further questionnaires. Garbo was also claiming expenses to go around the country visiting his agents. The truth was that not one of these agents existed, Garbo with Tommy Harris had made them all up. The Germans believed every word of these reports at the highest level.

On one occasion the Germans criticised one piece of information that was missing. Garbo had failed to report on a particular convoy from Liverpool. A plan to deal with this discrepancy was conjured up by Garbo and Tommy Harris and the W board. Garbo reported back that his agent in Liverpool was very ill, and in hospital. The local newspapers put a notice in that this particular person had died. Garbo sent this fabricated information back to the Germans, and they responded by sending money for the agent's family. Of course, the Liverpool agent, just like all the others, never existed. On another occasion Garbo informed the Germans of a notional convoy leaving Liverpool, the Germans dispatched a wolf pack of U-boats then at a later date their captains were disciplined for not finding the convoy. Garbo kept up this whole masquerade going right through to the end of the war. Juan Pujal Garcia, Agent Garbo, became our fifth D-day spy.

There were other double agents who should be mentioned whos stories are quite involved. Arthur Owens agent Snow, Wulf Schmidt agent Tate. Agents Zig Zag, also Mutt & Jeff and others who risked everything to assist the allied cause.

Fall of the *Abwehr*

It would appear that the *Abwehr*'s staff were not the vicious nasty murderers of the Nazi type. This was true as the *Abwehr* and the Nazis never quite saw eye to eye. It has been said that maybe the *Abwehr* suspected that their agents could possibly be fabricating and maybe even being controlled by the British. Some of the reports sent in were certainly padded out and exaggerated by the German handlers prior to being sent through to Berlin. We know this from the decrypts received at Bletchley Park, after all many Germans felt if Hitler loses the war it could only be a good thing for Germany. There was a joke circling around Germany at the time.

There was Hitler, Himmler, Goering, and Goebbels in an air raid shelter in Berlin. During an air raid the shelter received a direct hit. The shelter was blown apart who was saved?

The answer was Germany

It is also feasible that maybe the *Abwehr* reports that were coming in were further exaggerated, as this could mean Brownie points for that particular case officer, as it would be quite difficult to disprove a lot of these reports. At the end of the day it could cause that particular handler becoming out of favour with the Nazis, owing to a lack of information. The fear for the handler was being sent to the Russian front.

But this nice cosy club, all came tumbling down when two *Abwehr* officers in Turkey absconded to the allies. It was thought Dr. Erich and Elisabeth Vermehren were to be investigated in Berlin by the Gestapo for allegedly for spreading Nazi views. They knew what could be in store for them so they decided to try and defect to the allies, they contacted MI6 section V in Ankara. Nicolas Elliot who was the MI6 officer and head of station in Turkey, also a long standing friend of Kim Philby. Elliot assisted their escape to England via Cairo. Once in England they were to be housed temporarily at Kim Philby's mothers flat in Kensington. The Germans correctly believed that they took with them much top secret information. Hitler was furious; he summoned admiral Canaris the chief of the *Abwehr*. During the meeting a row ensued and Canaris was sacked. Hitler then ordered the complete *Abwehr* organisation to be disbanded. It was to be replaced by the SD (*Ausland Sicherheistdeinst)*, the security service for foreign countries. The SD were not pussycats they were the intelligence services of the SS and the Nazi party. But even with the new administration in force and much of the original organisation destroyed just enough remained in place that in many instances it was business as usual. The information coming through the British double cross system remained as false as it has had ever been.

Bodyguard

Britain was now controlling the complete German Intelligence system, with fabricated information created by the W Board to fool the Germans. We could monitor their reaction by intercepting and breaking their coded messages. The Germans believed all they were told, without exception. So it was now time to tell them about the invasion of Europe, D-day. They knew it was coming, but they did not know where or when. This was to be called "Operation Fortitude" the D-day deception plan. The Germans realised that, with the impending allied invasion of Europe, there would be some kind of deception plan involved. What actually happened, there were to be a number of deception plans in place. At the Tehran conference in 28th November 1943 to 1st December 1943, Churchill, Roosevelt and Stalin started to discuss the endgame of the war. Whereby plans were being made to reclaim Europe from the Nazis. All battles must be combined with a deception plan. It would appear obvious to the enemy that deception plans would be part of the operation. Therefore it was decided to have many deception plans to confuse the enemy. Churchill said "these plans must be protected by a bodyguard of lies" so the overall collection of deceptions became known as "Operation Bodyguard".

The main deceptions used, as part of Bodyguard, was the Atlantic invasion of Bordeaux, known as Operation Ironside, a seaborne operation consisting of two divisions from Britain and eight divisions direct from the USA. Fortitude North the invasion of north Norway by an army of 160,000 troops based at Edinburgh Castle, using the notional 4th British Army Group. Operation Fortitude South the invasion of Par de Calais by the First United States Army Group (FUSAG) commanded by General Patton. All of these armies were completely fabricated. Whilst we were aware that the Germans wouldn't be fooled by every deception, through our network of double-cross agents, we were going to make the Germans believe in three main possibilities. The real invasion, Operation Overlord, was planned to take place on the beaches of Normandy.

Our double-cross agents would continually send messages back to the *Abwehr*, telling of massive troop movements where there were none, and conversely where there was a buildup of troops, tanks and landing craft, we told the Germans that the road and towns were deserted. We invented two massive armies that did not exist "The First US army group" FUSAG, based in Kent with tens of thousands of troops ready to pounce on Calais at a moment's notice. To backup our double-agents stories, and in case of reconnaissance flights by the Germans, we built cardboard aircraft and rubber tanks all placed in the fields of Kent. Dummy radio messages were sent day and night to show a high level of military activity. We even gave the dummy army a real-life general, General Patton.

Meanwhile, in Scotland, another fake army was being mobilised, according to the information that our double-agents were sending to the Germans. The Forth British army Group (non-existent) was based at Edinburgh Castle. Mobilised and ready to invade Norway. This was Operation Fortitude North, which held back the 12th Panzer Division, supported as it was by *Luftwaffe*. Fortitude South, at Calais, held back the mighty 15th SS Panzer Division, which was commanded by General Erwin Rommel and Field Marshall von Rundstedt. Operation Ironside held back the 17th Panzer division. In charge of the military maneuvers for Operation Overlord, the real invasion at Normandy, was General D Eisenhower in command of the Supreme Headquarters of the Allied Expeditionary Forces (SHAEF). Our double-cross spies were continuing to send Germany "chicken-feed", and Hitler was believing all he was told. A date was set for the 5th June 1944, but due to bad weather D-day was postponed to the 6th June. General Eisenhower insisted that it was imperative that there should be no serious opposition to the landings for at least 48 hours. Our agents were working flat-out, telling the Germans "that there will be an imminent attack on Calais at any time now".

The invasion commenced at the Normandy beaches. Bletchley Park intercepted signals that confirmed that Hitler's generals, Rommel & von Rundstedt started moving heavy artillery from Calais towards Normandy. Agent Garbo sent an urgent message to the Germans: "Don't be fooled, Normandy is a diversion!" The message got to Hitler, who then ordered the 15th Panzer Division back to Calais rescinding the order to move West. Garbo and his fake agents continued to impress the Germans with his duff information. After D+26, one month after D-day, Hitler's generals started questioning the FUSAG invasion of Calais, but it took the Germans another four weeks to do anything about it. It was now far too late as the Expeditionary Force had now established a bridgehead, and built Mulberry harbours and were now moving inland. Hitler was now informed that the FUSAG group in Kent were now dispersing and that Normandy will be the main attack. We had to inform the Germans of this so they would keep faith in our double agents as there were to be future operations. Amazingly, Hitler was so impressed with the information that Garbo had given to the Germans. He awarded Arabel (Garbo) the Iron Cross 2nd Class.

Our D-day double-cross spies laid out the playing field so that Operation Overlord could be the success that it was. As such they saved the lives of thousands of allied service personnel by holding back Hitler's mighty Panzers, and giving General Eisenhower not just his 48 hours, but almost eight weeks. The work for our double-cross agents was not yet finished. There was to be more deception for the Germans regarding their deadliest weapons to date the V1 and V2 rockets that could have completely devastated London and possibly other British cities. The Third Reich never found out about how gullible they were.

We were nearly caught out.

Britain was almost caught out as well. At the very heart of the British Secret Service were five Russian Spies. They all worked for MI5 and MI6 and one even worked at the British Government's Ultra Top Secret code-breaking establishment at Bletchley Park. They were all very privy to the nations uppermost secrets, including the plans for D-day, also our double-cross system. They told the Russians everything. Of course, the Russians were then our allies, but remember that Hitler also had code-breakers. The Germans were breaking into Russian codes. We could have so easily had the plans for operation Overlord D-day and double-cross system compromised through the actions of these rogues, in the very highest echelons of our security services. It was an extremely close call and could have easily cost us the war. These highly respected individual continued to spy for the Russians into the 1950s during the Cold War. One almost became the Chief of MI6 "C" another became the advisor of art to HM Queen Elizabeth. These dreadful traitors included none other than Sir Anthony Blunt, Kim Philby, Guy Burgess, Donald Maclean, and John Cairncross. Burgess and Maclean defected to Moscow in 1951 following a tip-off from Philby. He defected himself in 1963. In 1979: Blunt was revealed as 'fourth man' The Prime Minister, Margaret Thatcher, named Sir Anthony Blunt, a former security service officer as the "fourth man" in the Cambridge spy ring. The fifth man John Cairncross did not consider that he was a spy he merely insisted that he was assisting the allies by passing them needed information that Stalin would not accept through normal channels. Especially that of the German decrypts of Operation Zitadelle the battle of the Kursk. Caincross was never prosecuted for treason as it was claimed that the information at that time was passed to an ally not an enemy. I am sure we are all aware that spying goes on today in Britain, not just military spying, but also commercial, infiltration of our businesses our factories, and of course the internet, sending information back to all corners of the world. Here are three things to remember: Regularly change your passwords for banking and internet. Most spies do it for the money, not for loyalty.

Finally, spies do not all go around looking like James Bond, shaken, but not stirred.

From Lorenz to Colossus the World's First Computer

During the Second World War the German army high command asked the Lorenz electronics company to manufacture for them a high security teleprinter cipher system to enable them to communicate by landline or radio in absolute secrecy. Lorenz Company designed a machine based on the additive method for enciphering teleprinter messages that had been invented in 1918 by Gilbert Vernam in America.

Bletchley Park was the British Government's Code-breaking centre during World War II the official name was the Government Code & Cipher School, or GC&CS. Often jokingly called the Golf Club and Chess Society, but normally just referred to as BP. The name "Station X" was normally used by people at other establishments who were authorised to know of its existence.

In previous chapters, we looked mainly at the German cipher machine Enigma. The Enigma was not only used by German military, but also by the Italians and the Japanese. However, there were many other ciphers which had to be broken during the war. There were hand ciphers, one-time pads, code-books of various types as well as many other machines including hand cipher drums, Haglin machines and the Japanese cipher machine (known as the purple machine).

The British were reading signals from the *Luftwaffe* (the German Air Force), the German army, navy and spy network *Abwehr*, as well as many other areas of enemy conflict. But with all this the signals were nearly all operational. There were no messages regarding strategic planning, no high-grade information from the *Oberkommando der Wehrmacht* (Hitler's desk). How was Hitler communicating with his generals?

In 1941, the Metropolitan Police operated a wireless intercept station at Denmark Hill in South London. This was based in some spare rooms in an old police nursing home. The Metropolitan police in conjunction with MI5 were on the lookout for subversive organsations which were using radio to communicate. The intercept station was keeping an eye especially on a Trotskyist plot to turn the world Communist. The Comintern organisation would attempt to infiltrate the trade unions, newspapers they were also trying to set up clandestine radio stations. Denmark Hill would scan the airwaves for the possibility of tracking down any Communist radio stations. One day while scanning the networks, another police intercept station on the south coast listening out for German spies picked up a new sound. It was like a very high-speed Morse code transmission.

The signal was not Morse, but believed to be a transmitted teleprinter signal. These transmissions became known as "non Morse". An attempt was made to connect the signal to a British teleprinter but to no avail. It was decided that the signal was too fast and incompatible. The only other way to read this signal was very slow and laborious, as you shall see. The received signal was recorded, using an ink pen recorder known as an undulator. The input would be the radio signal, and the output would be a paper-tape with a pen trace of the signal, this looked similar to a square-wave formation on a long slip of paper. It was possible, but long-winded, to identify the wave pattern on the tape as letters and numbers. Whoever was sending this signal was using the Baudate Murray five-bit teleprinter code. The coded text could then be extracted. It could then be punched onto five-hole teleprinter tape.

Further investigations were made by the GPO direction-finding team which established that these signals were coming from Central and Eastern Europe, some were probably emanating from Germany. The coded text, known as cipher text, along with these tapes was sent to Bletchley Park by dispatch rider, where a special section was set up to deal with this new concept. Major Ralph Tester was an accountant working for Unilever before the war. At the outbreak of conflict, he worked for the BBC monitoring service as he was fluent in the German language. During 1941, he was recruited to Bletchley Park. After several specialist code-breaking positions, he was asked to head his own section: the department known as the "Testery" Along with Captain Jerry Roberts and others, they were looking at these new ciphers that appeared to be emanating from German high-speed teleprinters. The tapes would be received from Denmark Hill on a regular basis. The decrypting of these was going to become a tremendous issue, as staff and resources were thrown at the problem.

Due to the increasing volume of these non-Morse signals, a new Y-station (wireless intercept station) was set up at Knockhalt in Kent, close to Sevenoaks. This was to be run by the Foreign office. This station was headed by Harold Kenworthy, previously of Denmark Hill. It was operated by teams of ATS girls, who would intercept the signals, feed them through the undulator machines, to produce the paper slip, which would then in turn be punched onto the five-hole teleprinter tape "Just like that". The procedure sounds simple but was in fact a horrendously long-winded and boring task. The ATS girls did a fantastic job, sending the punched tapes on their way by dispatch riders on fast motorbikes to the Testery at Bletchley Park. The breaking of this particular cipher was beginning to make the Enigma machine look like a piece of apple pie.

The Testery team was not aware at this stage that there were two different machines sending these signals. These machines were being used by the Germans to send the high-grade messages that we were missing. The Lorenz SZ40/42 was being used by the *Oberkommando der Wehrmacht* and by Adolf Hitler himself to send battle-plans and high grade traffic to his generals. This was the machine that we had to break at all costs. The other non-Morse teleprinter, used by the *Oberkommando der Luftwaffe*, Supreme Commander of the German air force Herman Goering, was the Siemens T52. As we were already breaking into the *Luftwaffe* Enigma *red code* on a daily basis it was no need to commit any time and resources on this particular machine.

Lorenz SZ 40/42 Cipher attachment
With kind permission Bletchley Park Trust

These machines were known as "cipher attachments". Manufactured by Lorenz and Siemens, both were German electronics companies which made teleprinters. The teleprinter operator would type out the message; it would then be passed through the cipher attachments to encrypt the message automatically. Once encrypted, the message was transmitted.

At the other end of the network, a recipient operator would receive the signal via his cipher attachment. Providing his settings were correct the message would be deciphered automatically and printed out ready to read.

The sender operator sent his message in plain text and it was encrypted and decrypted automatically by the machines. The receiving operator then received his message in plain text, all much quicker than the Enigma system that required three operators at each end.

In the earlier part of the war these signals were sent over telephone lines, which would have been very difficult to hack into in an enemy country. This was the reason that the British were unaware of this system up to now. However, as the Germans invaded more distant lands, they were forced to use radio links for these communications. As soon as they used radio for sending non-Morse transmissions, the British Y-stations intercepted them. These were the signals that Denmark Hill had originally been receiving. We know that Bletchley Park had no idea what these machines were called, but they were very good at giving things names. The Enigma networks were given colours red/blue/light blue etc. The non-Morse signals were given the names of fish because we knew through our Intelligence sources that the Germans called one of their teleprinter cipher systems "*Sagefish*" ("Sawfish"). Bletchley Park called the Siemans & Halske T52 "Sturgeon" and the Lorenz SZ40/42 "Tunny". It must be emphasised that Bletchley Park had never seen these machines or knew what they were called. They only had the teleprinter tapes and the print-out that Denmark Hill and Knockhalt had sent them.

At this stage, the Testery department was without success. Resources, time and money were being poured into what looked like a completely impossible task. Commander Edward Travis, who was now the chief at Bletchley Park, was looking very closely at the pennies, and considering whether it was time to call it a day, so that resources could be better used elsewhere. However in the nick of time, the Germans made a historic blunder, and the breakthrough came.

The Big mistake.

On the 30th August 1941, a signal was intercepted at Denmark Hill. It was a message containing 3976 characters. The pre-amble which was the wheel settings for each of the twelve wheels, was always sent in plain text. This enabled the recipient operator to set his machine wheels to the same settings. On this occasion it was HQIBPEXEZMUG. Firstly, the Germans should have known to keep their messages short for security. The message was sent from Vienna to Athens. After the message was sent, a plain text reply was sent back to Vienna from Athens that stated "Message corrupted send again". If an identical message had been re-sent, it would not have helped the code-breakers at all. The operator in Vienna could not have been best pleased as he would have had to re-type almost 4000 characters. His correct procedure before re-sending a message should have been to reset the ten pin-wheels of his Lorenz machine. He obviously failed to comply with these strict operating instructions. The operator was clearly slack or lazy, this one breach with his failure to adhere to the regulations set a chain reaction that changed the history of code-breaking forever. He used the same wheel settings HQIBPEXEZMUG then re-typed the message, including many abbreviations and spelling mistakes, making the text almost four-hundred characters shorter. The operator probably thought, as this is only a test message that it didn't matter and no one would be listening anyway. The fact was the whole world was listening to him.

To summarise, the same message was sent on the same settings with 10% fewer characters. The code-breakers had struck gold. Denmark Hill who, upon receipt of the signal, very soon realised that it was a double-send. Dispatch riders were hastily on their way to Bletchley Park, and the Testery was on stand-by. These precious tapes and transcript were handed to Brigadier John Tiltman, probably one of the finest code-breakers who ever lived. He could crack Japanese codes, and he also spoke many languages. Tiltman was known to prefer to work standing up at a high desk to sitting. He soon established that whatever machine was being used had adapted the Vernam Cipher, which uses a procedure of adding characters together, and it took him just two weeks to extract the plain text from the encrypted tapes.

So now we had an insight into their system, from now on referred to as "Tunny". However, not all messages would have been sent in duplicate. The next stage would be to work out the structure of the Tunny system. One of the members of the research team at Bletchley Park was William Tutte, a Chemistry and Maths graduate from Trinity College Cambridge. Bill Tutte was given the tapes and asked to investigate the workings of the machines. Just a few weeks later, he returned to the Testery and said "I don't know who makes this machine or what it is called, but I do know how it works". Tutte established the structural workings of the Lorenz SZ40/42 or "Tunny" without ever seeing the machine. Just from the two tapes and some mathematics. Then Tutte profoundly stated: "We can build one". So plans were drawn up.

With the assistance of the General Post Office Research station at Dollis hill, North London. The Tunny machine was built. The difference being that the actual Lorenz machine had 12 rotors or pinwheels, as they became known. Tutte's Tunny machine would have 12 rows of small lamps to mimic the functions of the wheels. So you might conclude that we had cracked Hitler's most secret cipher machine, but it was still taking five to six weeks to break a single message, this was far too long to be of any use.

Undulator Ink Pen Recorder
With kind permission of The National Museum Computing

We were now receiving many more punched tapes from Knockhalt Y-station; at this stage we were still unable to establish the settings of the Tunny (Lorenz) rotors. That was the crucial problem. Alan Turning had been away in the United States working with the Bell Telephone company, as well as with National Cash Registers, on vital cipher equipment. Turing returned to Bletchley Park in his new role as general consultant. He became involved in the Tunny problem. They knew that the German machine had a cam wheel. Turing established a procedure for working out the wheel's turn-over point.This method became known as "Turingismus".

The Testary employed many other brilliant people: Peter Hilton, who became a Professor of Mathematics; Donald Michie; Jack Good; and many others including Max Newman, who happened to be one of Alan Turing's lecturers when he was at King's College Cambridge. But even with all these people it was still taking approximately six weeks to break a code from Tunny. Max Newman realised that the whole system could be sped up by introducing machines that would do a large part of the job. If a machine could be invented to obtain the position of the first five rotors of the Tunny, the remainder of the rotor positions could easily be worked out by hand. A machine would cost money to build, initiate, run and maintain, there was also the question of the number of staff required to operate it. This was starting to look like a whole new department. Max Newman approached Commander Edward Travis who was already concerned over the costs of the Testary with its lack of results. With the increasing costs in personnel involved in a project that seemed to be stagnating, Travis was not impressed. All we can say is that knowing Travis, Newman must have done one hell of a good job "to put forward his case for more resources". It was agreed that Max Newman should head his own department to mechanise the breaking of Tunny.

The Tunny Machine emulated Lorenz SZ 40/42

With kind permission of The National Museum Computing

The department in block H at Bletchley Park would be known as the Newmanry. Newman contacted an old friend and colleague of his from his Cambridge days, Charles Eryl Wynn-Williams, a Welsh physicist. He was best known for his work at the Cavendish Laboratory at Cambridge, using thermionic values for counting atomic Alpha particles. In 1935, Wynn-Williams lectured in physics at Imperial College London, and during the war he worked towards the development of radar at the Telecommunications Research Establishment (TRE) in Malvern, Worcestershire. He had already been working in conjunction with Bletchley Park on other projects, so he was asked again to assist. The problems with Tunny basically were counting issues. There were billions of more possibilities of code combinations in Tunny compared to Enigma, and this had become a problem of a colossal magnitude. Wynn-Williams and the TRE along with the Dollis Hill Post Office Research establishment, came up with a machine. The new invention used radio valves for high speed calculations, utilising electronics as opposed to mechanical relays this increased speed a million-fold. The machine, known as the Robinson, used two-teleprinter tapes. One was the original message tape, whilst the other consisted of sequencing data. The two tapes were looped and pulled around a pulley of sprocket wheels at high speed. With the use of an optical light sensor, the Robinson machine could read data at a thousand characters per second. All this was built onto what looked like a vertical iron bedstead.

The Robinson
With kind permission of The National Museum Computing

The Robinson machine worked. It could read the data and reduce the breaking of the Tunny code from five or six weeks (by hand), to two or three weeks by machine. However, there were some serious issues with it. The early machines overheated, causing resistors to emit clouds of noxious smoke. Its effectiveness was greatly affected by humidity and the amount of moisture in the air. If damp, the tapes would tend to stretch, giving thoroughly inaccurate readings. However, if the air was warm and dry, the tape was susceptible to breaking, sending streams of high-speed punched tape all over the machine and the surrounding floor. Very soon, the Wrens who operated the Robinsons renamed them the "Heath

172

Robinson", named for the cartoonist at the time, famed for drawing pictures of machines that could not possibly work.

There were several Robinsons operating. It was becoming obvious that this was not the answer. Max Newman again consulted Alan Turing to see what could be done to improve the situation. Turing had some knowledge of machines that worked with radio valves, as some of his work was with the Bell Telephone Company in the USA. This had brought him in contact with the British Research Telecommunications engineers at the GPO Dollis Hill. Turing advised Newman to have a chat with the senior engineer Thomas (Tommy) Flowers. Flowers was working with thermionic valves in telephone circuits. He was developing methods that would speed up trunk dialing systems. Once Flowers understood Newman's problems, he came up with a plan for the machine. The new machine that Flowers had invented would require 1500 radio valves. It would only require the original message tape. This one tape would have to run at a much faster speed. To avoid the tape breaking, instead of using sprocket wheels to pull the tape through the machine, Flowers would use spring-loaded pulleys to maintain the correct tension on the tapes.

Tests were performed with the tape running at an equivalent speed of thirty miles per hour without breaking. This new machine could read data at 5,000 characters per second. Initially, Tommy Flowers was asked how long the machine would take to build. He believed that it would take eighteen months, but the authorities at Bletchley Park weren't too keen to fund the project for that length of time. They told Flowers that they would be continuing with the Robinsons machines and they would start to order more of them. Flowers was devastated, and knew that his own machine would work. He spoke to his engineering colleagues and the team decided to build the new machine themselves. Flowers was so convinced that his giant machine would solve the problems that Bletchley Park had encountered with the Tunny codes.

Therefore Flowers decided partly finance the project himself. Flowers and his team, in their own time, worked around the clock realising the importance of what they were building. The machine was ready and tested in December 1943, it was installed at Bletchley Park in January 1944. This colossal machine became known as Colossus. In February 1943 Colossus did its first job. It worked first time. Colossus could detect the position of the first five pinwheels of the Tunny (Lorenz SZ40/42) not in six weeks or even three weeks, but in six hours. Colossus would read data at 5,000 characters per second; with parallel and switched programming it could eliminate the trillions of possibilities. Once located, the Tunny wheel position results would be printed out on an electric writer. Then they would be sent to the Testery where the positions of the remainder of the wheels would be calculated manually. This would enable them to set up the lamp-board on our Tunny machines, which mimicked Lorenz. The original message tape would be passed through our Tunny machine which was attached to a teleprinter then, like magic, out comes the plain German text. The whole operation is completed in six and a half hours.

Colossus Mk1. 1944
'© Crown. Reproduced by kind permission, Director, GCHQ

Whether Tommy Flowers ever got his money back, we just don't know, probably not. Though in later life, he did receive an MBE. Due to the secrecy of his work, and the impending cold war with the Soviet Union, he was basically unrewarded for his work. There were eventually ten Colossus machines at Bletchley Park, the mark II version contained 2,500 valves. Flowers was criticised heavily for using radio valves, considering their reputation for unreliability. He knew the weak point of valves in radios, due to the radio being switched on and off. But as far as Colossus was concerned, once it was switched on, it stayed on for the rest of the war. I am glad I wasn't paying the electric bill, each machine burns 5.5kW of electricity per hour!

The Colossus machines were installed in the most important year of the war. The preparations were being made for the largest land invasion in the history of the world. It was planned that the first day of what was to become Operation Overlord, or D-Day, would involve 156,000 men, 1,500 tanks, 6,939 ships of various types, including support vessels, 11,590 aircraft. All to be followed by a further three million service personnel. Hitler spoke to his generals before, during and after the event. Bletchley Park was always listening to his plans. D-Day was a deception, months of careful planning called Operation Fortitude North and Fortitude South. The plan was to make Hitler believe the allies would invade Norway from Scotland, also to attack Calais in France, where the English Channel was at its narrowest point of just twenty-one miles wide.

The Allies intended to really invade the Normandy beaches. The deception was to use "Double Cross" agents to feed disinformation to the Germans. Also to deceive the Germans to believe we had a massive army in Kent ready to pounce on Calais at any moment. We needed to hear Hitler's plans. Those secret plans and orders were sent to his generals using the Lorenz teleprinters which were each connected to the Lorenz SZ40/42 cipher attachment. Those signals were then sent by radio, which was subsequently intercepted.

Just prior to D-Day, receiving aerials were erected at Bletchley Park to speed up the intercept and code-breaking process. The Colossus machines were now deciphering messages going to and coming from Hitler within just a few hours of being sent. It has been said in jest, by one code-breaker that "if Hitler wants his messages any quicker, he should just telephone Bletchley Park!"

The European war ended on May 8th 1945 after ten months of heavy fighting across France and Germany. Prior to Berlin being entered by the allies, Adolf Hitler, along with a proportion of his cronies, committed suicide on 30th April. In the absence of Grossadmiral Karl Doenitz, Hitler's deputy, the surrender was signed by Colonel General Alfred Jodl at Reims, France on 7 May 1945. The war in the East dragged on for a further three months.

Post war

At Bletchley Park, redundancies had already begun, with many of the brilliant minds going back into academia. Many went on to the new Government Communication Headquarters at Eastcote, Middlesex, (and later to Cheltenham) whilst the rest were given a thank you and goodbye, similar to many people in our armed services.

Orders came through to destroy all the documents and dismantle the machinery. These secret people were then reminded that should they ever murmur a word of their work at Bletchley, they would face the most severe consequences, they then disappeared as if they had never existed.

With the destruction and dismantling of equipment the remaining two Colossus machines eventually found their way to the new GCHQ at Cheltenham. The question is why? It has been suggested, but never confirmed that when the Russians fought their way across Poland to Germany, they would have overrun the German communication posts. Therefore it was conceivable that the Russians would have picked up any cipher equipment they could have laid their hands on including Lorenz.

The thoughts behind this were that the Russians could possibly use this equipment in a possible future conflict. Therefore, our security services could be one step ahead. It must be pointed out that this theory has been vehemently denied by GCHQ, the listening arm of the security service. They stated that the Colossus machines were purely used for statistical purposes. The last two Colossus machines were scrapped in 1960 the plans were burnt and its very existence was kept secret.

After the war, Bletchley Park closed down, and eventually became a home for the General Post Office (GPO) Telephone Engineering Training School, and also housed the Civil Aviation Authority. There were other Government-based organisations also on site. However, it was absolutely certain that no one knew of what went on at Bletchley Park during the war years.

Tommy flowers the inventor of Colossus, was awarded £1000 as the majority of the original Colossus was paid for by himself. In latter years he assisted with the design and build of a machine called Ernie, (electronic random number indicating equipment) it was the machine that chose the numbers for premium Bond winners.

In 1974 a book was published by Group Captain Frederick Winterbotham, titled "The Ultra secret". This was the first British publication that would reveal the secrets of Bletchley Park during the war years. Winterbotham was the Chief of the Air Department of the Secret Intelligence Services (MI6) from 1930 until 1945. He worked in Hut 3 at Bletchley Park.

Although the book itself has discrepancies, he wrote about what he knew, or what he believed of the workings within the confines of Bletchley Park. So the cat was out of the bag, so to speak. Winterbotham even got away with breaking the thirty-year rule on top-secret intelligence matters; even though the book was published just a little shy of thirty years from the end of the war.

It was quite soon that newspapers started picking up the story of Bletchley Park. Magazine articles followed, along with TV, radio etc.

A senior lecturer of Computer Science at Newcastle University was in the process of writing a book on the origins of digital computers. Prof. Brian Randell had already discovered the early history up until 1939 including the work of Alan Turing in 1936 with his landmark paper on computable numbers. Then there was more information available after 1945, but nothing during the war years! After World War II there were digital computers, before the war, there was only the mathematics available. So it was becoming obvious to Brian Randell that there was work on computers during the war. Eventually, after a long struggle, previously secret information was released on Colossus. It was then possible for Professor Randell to complete his book of the "Origins of digital Computers, selected papers".

Enter Tony Sale

After National Service in the RAF, Tony Sale worked for the Marconi Company where he was an assistant to Peter Wright, on research into Doppler Radar. Wright was to become the future author of the controversial book "Spycatcher" which talks of Wright's work whilst at MI5. Sale followed Wright into MI5, and worked as a Senior Technical Officer. After various jobs in the Electronics & Weapons industry, Sale became a senior Curator at the London Science Museum. His job was to lead teams in the rebuilding of historic digital computers such as Pegasus. In 1991, he was part of a small group which began a campaign to save Bletchley Park for the nation.

It was just about the time that British Telecom, formerly "Post Office Telephones" Had pulled out of the old wartime code-breaking establishment and started to destroy the buildings. BT were making proposals to demolish the grand old mansion house, dig up the beautiful gardens, and sell the land. There was a public outcry, with a protest to BT and the government who jointly owned the site. In 1992 the Bletchley

Park Trust was formed. The Trust secured twenty nine acres of land, including the buildings which were left, along with the Victorian mansion house on a 250 year lease. Tony Sale having been familiar with the work of Prof Brian Randell and his research into digital computers knew all about the work of Colossus, he realised that it must have been the world's first electronic digital computer. Tony was convinced that Colossus could be re-built. In 1993, just one year after the formation of the Bletchley Park Trust, work began on the Colossus Rebuild project.

Wartime Bletchley Park started in 1939, code-breakers and ancillary staff started in the mansion house then a succession of wooden huts started to appear. As hundreds of staff turned into thousands, more work space had to be found. Following this, brick blocks were built to house even more staff, along with machinery. Two of these blocks, known as Blocks G and H, in wartime were used to house Colossus computers. The surviving H block was to be used by Tony Sale for the rebuild project. The big question was where to start. Tony managed to track down Tommy Flowers who was the designer and builder of the original Colossus back in 1943, some fifty years earlier. Though Tommy never kept any of his wartime documents, some of Tommy's engineering colleagues who also worked on the original Colossus were contacted. They had illegally kept some of the notes, plans and circuit diagrams. Also they discovered a set of eight original black and white photographs. They all gathered around Tony Sale's CAD (computer-aided design) machine and re-designed Colossus.

To be a genuine re-build, Tony realised that he would require a large proportion of original parts, but as you know, you can't just turn up at your local hardware store and expect them to have parts for Colossus in stock! However, there was some good luck to come into this story. Whilst all this was happening British Telecom were decommissioning their old analogue telephone exchanges and re-installing new digital systems. Remember Tommy Flowers worked at the Dollis Hill which was primarily a telephone exchange. The parts that were stored at Dollis Hill were readily available at every telephone exchange in the country. Essentially Tony Sale had to find out which exchange was converting to the new system, call them up and ask what they were doing with their old stuff! Hey, it was recycling, and they were more than happy for Tony to back up his truck and relieve them of their junk. The re-build of Colossus took fourteen years with a dedicated team of twenty volunteer electronics engineers and computer technicians. Then finally Colossus was ready to roll. The machine was tested and it worked. In 2007, visitors who came to Bletchley Park Museum could see Colossus the world's first computer working and reading data at 5,000 characters per second using a switched program logic system. It was a really great day for Tony Sale. There was a part switch-on in 2004, performed by the Duke of Kent, also in attendance that day was Tommy Flowers, who saw his invention Colossus run again as it had done sixty years before. But in 2007 Tony Sale had another issue, namely convincing Park visitors that this was not a mere "mock up". So to prove that this was a genuine working machine, Tony organised "The World Cipher Challenge". In the museum at Bletchley Park, there is a Lorenz Cipher machine SZ40/42, on loan from GCHQ Cheltenham. The machine was originally the property of WW2 German General Kesselring when he was captured in Berlin in 1945. Now it was in its full working order Tony wanted to send this machine back to Germany.

The idea was to send it to the Heinz Nixdorf Computer Museum in Paderborn, where Tony had some friends working. Special permissions had to be granted from GCHQ. We did not want the Germans pulling an "Elgin Marbles" on us, the Germans claiming ownership of the machine," because it's German!" Special permissions were granted and the Heinz Nixdorf Museum set up the Lorenz machine as it would have been done during the war. Signals were sent on this occasion by amateur radio, and could have been received anywhere in the world. Many computer geeks and enthusiasts were on standby, listening in for transmission. Tony Sale, along with his team, were waiting in the radio receiving room in Block H at Bletchley Park, and then they received their radio transmission. The acquired messages were put through the undulator then punched onto Five-hole teleprinter tape. Eventually these were taken to Colossus and looped around the pulleys.

In just three-and-a-half hours Tony and his team had broken the code that had been received from Germany. Soon afterwards, Tony sent a message to the world, asking if anyone could beat his time. It didn't take long for a reply to come through. It was from Joachim Schueth, a German professional computer software engineer, working on high-level Pentium processors who had written some special software that enabled him to break the code in just 46 seconds! But Joachim did state that he was reading data at 1.2 million characters per second. But to conclude five thousand Characters per second with the equivalent clock speed of 5.8MHz was truly a momentous achievement when Colossus was first tested at Dollis Hill in 1943.

This only goes to prove that Colossus was the world's first electronic digital computer, which beat the Americans, with their ENIAC machine, by almost two years. But they weren't to know this, as Colossus was a secret for over thirty years after the war.

Her Majesty the Queen visited Bletchley Park, and viewed the Colossus machine on 15th July 2011. Her main reason for the visit, was to unveil a memorial to the code-breakers and staff who worked there during World War II the memorial reads "We Also Served".

Just six weeks later, on the 28th August, broke the tragic news of Tony Sale's sudden death. Tony had always been proud to tell the world that Colossus the first electronic digital computer was British!

Colossus is now housed in Block H at the National Museum of Computing at Bletchley Park.

Glossary

ASDIC	Anti-Submarine detection Committee
ATS	Auxiliary Territorial Services
C	Chief of MI6
DNI	Director of Naval Intelligence
GC&CS	Government Code & Cipher School
GCHQ	Gov. Communications Head Quarters
MI 1b	WW1 Army Codebreaking Section
MI5	Defense of the realm, Home security
MI5 B	Counter-subversion
MI5 B1a	Double agent section
MI6	see SIS
NID	Naval Intelligence Department
OIC	Operational Intelligence Centre (Admiralty House London)
PWE	Political Warfare Executive
RAF	Royal Air force
SIS	Secret Intelligence Service (MI6).
ULTRA	Decrypted messages from Bletchley Park
WAFS	Women's Auxiliary Air Force
WRNS	(Wrens) Women's Royal Naval Service

Bibliography

1939	Richard Overy
30 Secret Years	Robin Denniston
Action This Day	Michael Smith
Alan Turing the Enigma	Andrew Hodges
Battle for the Code	Hugh Sebag Montefiore
Bismarck 1941	Angus Konstam
Black Boomerang	Dennis Sefton Delmer
Britain's Best Kept Secret	Ted Enever
British Intelligence in the Second World War	F H Hinsley
Capturing Enigma	Stephen Harper
Code-Breakers	Hinsley & Stripp
Code Book	Simon Singh
Colossus	Jack Copeland
Colossus 1943 - 1996	Tony Sale
Colossus BP's greatest secret	Michael Smith
Defence of the Realm	Christopher Andrew
Discovery of the Bismarck	Robert Ballard
Double Cross	Ben Macintyre
Finest Years	Max Hastings
GCHQ	Richard Aldrich
Hut 6 Story	Gordon Welchman

183

Kriegsmarine U-Boats	Gordon Williamson
MI6 History of	Keith Jeffrey
Pursuit	Ludovic Kennedy
Room 39	Donald McLachlan
Second World War	S.P. MacKenzie
Secret History of PWE	David Garnett
Secret Life of BP	Sinclair McKay
Secret War	Michael Smith
Secret Wireless War	Geoffrey Pidgeon
Seizing the Enigma	David Kahn
Sigint	Peter Matthews
The Secret of Station X	Michael Smith
Ultra Secret	Fred Winterbotham
Wolfpack	David Jordan
World War 2	John Keegan